An Analysis of

Homi K. Bhabha's

The Location of
Culture

Stephen Fay
with
Liam Haydon

Published by Macat International Ltd
24:13 Coda Centre, 189 Munster Road, London SW6 6AW.

Distributed exclusively by Routledge
2 Park Square, Milton Park, Abingdon, Oxon OX14 4RN
711 Third Avenue, New York, NY 10017, USA

Routledge is an imprint of the Taylor & Francis Group, an informa business

www.macat.com
info@macat.com

Cataloguing in Publication Data
A catalogue record for this book is available from the British Library.
Library of Congress Cataloguing-in-Publication Data is available upon request.
Cover illustration: Kim Thompson

ISBN 978-1-912302-82-6 (hardback)
ISBN 978-1-912127-27-6 (paperback)
ISBN 978-1-912281-70-1 (e-book)

Notice
The information in this book is designed to orientate readers of the work under analysis,
to elucidate and contextualise its key ideas and themes, and to aid in the development
of critical thinking skills. It is not meant to be used, nor should it be used, as a
substitute for original thinking or in place of original writing or research. References and
notes are provided for informational purposes and their presence does not constitute
endorsement of the information or opinions therein. This book is presented solely for
educational purposes. It is sold on the understanding that the publisher is not engaged
to provide any scholarly advice. The publisher has made every effort to ensure that
this book is accurate and up-to-date, but makes no warranties or representations with
regard to the completeness or reliability of the information it contains. The information
and the opinions provided herein are not guaranteed or warranted to produce particular
results and may not be suitable for students of every ability. The publisher shall not be
liable for any loss, damage or disruption arising from any errors or omissions, or from
the use of this book, including, but not limited to, special, incidental, consequential or
other damages caused, or alleged to have been caused, directly or indirectly, by the
information contained within.

CONTENTS

WAYS IN TO THE TEXT

Who Is Homi K. Bhabha?   9
What Does *The Location of Culture* Say?   10
Why Does *The Location of Culture* Matter?   12

SECTION 1: INFLUENCES

Module 1: The Author and the Historical Context   15
Module 2: Academic Context   20
Module 3: The Problem   25
Module 4: The Author's Contribution   30

SECTION 2: IDEAS

Module 5: Main Ideas   35
Module 6: Secondary Ideas   40
Module 7: Achievement   45
Module 8: Place in the Author's Work   50

SECTION 3: IMPACT

Module 9: The First Responses   55
Module 10: The Evolving Debate   59
Module 11: Impact and Influence Today   64
Module 12: Where Next?   68

Glossary of Terms   73
People Mentioned in the Text   78
Works Cited   84

THE MACAT LIBRARY

The Macat Library is a series of unique academic explorations of seminal works in the humanities and social sciences – books and papers that have had a significant and widely recognised impact on their disciplines. It has been created to serve as much more than just a summary of what lies between the covers of a great book. It illuminates and explores the influences on, ideas of, and impact of that book. Our goal is to offer a learning resource that encourages critical thinking and fosters a better, deeper understanding of important ideas.

Each publication is divided into three Sections: Influences, Ideas, and Impact. Each Section has four Modules. These explore every important facet of the work, and the responses to it.

This Section-Module structure makes a Macat Library book easy to use, but it has another important feature. Because each Macat book is written to the same format, it is possible (and encouraged!) to cross-reference multiple Macat books along the same lines of inquiry or research. This allows the reader to open up interesting interdisciplinary pathways.

To further aid your reading, lists of glossary terms and people mentioned are included at the end of this book (these are indicated by an asterisk [*] throughout) – as well as a list of works cited.

Macat has worked with the University of Cambridge to identify the elements of critical thinking and understand the ways in which six different skills combine to enable effective thinking.
Three allow us to fully understand a problem; three more give us the tools to solve it. Together, these six skills make up the **PACIER** model of critical thinking. They are:

ANALYSIS – understanding how an argument is built
EVALUATION – exploring the strengths and weaknesses of an argument
INTERPRETATION – understanding issues of meaning

CREATIVE THINKING – coming up with new ideas and fresh connections
PROBLEM-SOLVING – producing strong solutions
REASONING – creating strong arguments

To find out more, visit **WWW.MACAT.COM.**

CRITICAL THINKING AND *THE LOCATION OF CULTURE*

Primary critical thinking skill: INTERPRETATION
Secondary critical thinking skill: CREATIVE THINKING

Homi K. Bhabha's 1994 *The Location of Culture* is one of the founding texts of the branch of literary theory called postcolonialism.

While postcolonialism has many strands, at its heart lies the question of interpreting and understanding encounters between the western colonial powers and the nations across the globe that they colonized. Colonization was not just an economic, military or political process, but one that radically affected culture and identity across the world. It is a field in which interpretation comes to the fore, and much of its force depends on addressing the complex legacy of colonial encounters by careful, sustained attention to the meaning of the traces that they left on colonized cultures.

What Bhabha's writing, like so much postcolonial thought, shows is that the arts of clarification and definition that underpin good interpretation are rarely the same as simplification. Indeed, good interpretative clarification is often about pointing out and dividing the different kinds of complexity at play in a single process or term. For Bhabha, the object is identity itself, as expressed in the ideas colonial powers had about themselves. In his interpretation, what at first seems to be the coherent set of ideas behind colonialism soon breaks down into a complex mass of shifting stances – yielding something much closer to postcolonial thought than a first glance at his sometimes dauntingly complex suggests.

ABOUT THE AUTHOR OF THE ORIGINAL WORK

Homi K. Bhabha was born in Mumbai, India, in 1949 into the minority Parsi community, and went on to study and work in the United Kingdom and the United States, factors that have contributed to his interest in the things that lie in between cultures. Completing postgraduate studies at Oxford University, Bhabha forged a career in academia in both the UK and the US, while also advising important organizations such as the World Economic Forum and UNESCO, the United Nations Educational Scientific and Cultural Organization. Bhabha's key work, *The Location of Culture* (1994), has seen him recognized as one of the founding fathers of what is known as postcolonial studies.

ABOUT THE AUTHORS OF THE ANALYSIS

Dr Stephen Fay holds a doctorate in Hispanic studies from University College, London. His research focuses on ideas of national culture and identity in twentieth-century Cuba. He currently teaches Spanish literature and translation at University College, London.

Dr Liam Haydon holds a doctorate in English literature from Manchester University. He is currently a postdoctoral researcher at the University of Kent, where his work focuses on the cultural impacts of global trade in the early seventeenth century.

ABOUT MACAT

GREAT WORKS FOR CRITICAL THINKING

Macat is focused on making the ideas of the world's great thinkers accessible and comprehensible to everybody, everywhere, in ways that promote the development of enhanced critical thinking skills.

It works with leading academics from the world's top universities to produce new analyses that focus on the ideas and the impact of the most influential works ever written across a wide variety of academic disciplines. Each of the works that sit at the heart of its growing library is an enduring example of great thinking. But by setting them in context – and looking at the influences that shaped their authors, as well as the responses they provoked – Macat encourages readers to look at these classics and game-changers with fresh eyes. Readers learn to think, engage and challenge their ideas, rather than simply accepting them.

'Macat offers an amazing first-of-its-kind tool for interdisciplinary learning and research. Its focus on works that transformed their disciplines and its rigorous approach, drawing on the world's leading experts and educational institutions, opens up a world-class education to anyone.'

Andreas Schleicher
Director for Education and Skills, Organisation for Economic Co-operation and Development

'Macat is taking on some of the major challenges in university education ... They have drawn together a strong team of active academics who are producing teaching materials that are novel in the breadth of their approach.'

Prof Lord Broers,
former Vice-Chancellor of the University of Cambridge

'The Macat vision is exceptionally exciting. It focuses upon new modes of learning which analyse and explain seminal texts which have profoundly influenced world thinking and so social and economic development. It promotes the kind of critical thinking which is essential for any society and economy. This is the learning of the future.'

Rt Hon Charles Clarke, former UK Secretary of State for Education

'The Macat analyses provide immediate access to the critical conversation surrounding the books that have shaped their respective discipline, which will make them an invaluable resource to all of those, students and teachers, working in the field.'

Professor William Tronzo, University of California at San Diego

WAYS IN TO THE TEXT

KEY POINTS

- Homi Bhabha (b. 1949) is an Indian academic and postcolonial* theorist (postcolonialism is an academic discipline concerned with uncovering and criticizing the various cultural, political, and social legacies of colonial rule).
- *The Location of Culture* (1994) argues that there is no such thing as a stable identity* (that is, roughly, an unchanging "personhood" or sense of self).
- The text is one of the founding works of postcolonial thought.

Who Is Homi Bhabha?

Homi K. Bhabha, the author of *The Location of Culture* (1994), was born in the Indian city of Mumbai in 1949. He is a member of an Indian minority group, the Parsi,* a community descended from refugees from present-day Iran that continues to maintain a degree of ethnic separation even today. While his experience as someone between cultures may well have affected his writings, Bhabha himself rarely makes reference to his background or upbringing.

Bhabha attended a private school and university in Mumbai, before moving to Oxford for his postgraduate work. He has since been employed as an academic in the United Kingdom and United

States. Most of the essays that make up *The Location of Culture* were written during Bhabha's time as a lecturer at the University of Sussex.

The Location of Culture cemented Bhabha's growing reputation in the field of postcolonial theory, a discipline concerned with the various legacies of the colonial period. He has received many awards and fellowships, including at the universities of Princeton and Pennsylvania. In 1997 he moved to the University of Chicago, and in 2001 he was made the Anne F. Rothburg Professor of Literature at Harvard University.

Now a prominent and influential academic, Bhabha has advised the World Economic Forum (an international institution founded to further cooperation between the state-owned and private spheres) and UNESCO* (United Nations Educational Scientific and Cultural Organization, a global institution founded with the aim of promoting peace through international collaboration in areas such as science, culture, and education) on how to reduce poverty and inequality. He also serves as part of the Asian Art Council for the Guggenheim museum in New York.

What Does *The Location of Culture* Say?

The Location of Culture is a series of challenges to the concept of identity. It takes as its starting point that in the West there has been a fundamental division into "West" and "East" or, more generally, "Other."* By "Other," Bhabha (and other postcolonial writers) means something that is seen as different from, and often inferior to, the "Self." So, in the case of West and East, Bhabha builds on the work of the Palestinian American thinker Edward Said,* who argued that the West sees itself positively as cultured, civilized, and industrious, and the East as prone to self-indulgent pleasure, lazy, and uncivilized.

Bhabha aimed to show that binary divisions like East–West were unstable and unsustainable and he developed two key concepts, hybridity* and mimicry,* in order to do so. Hybridity is the idea that identities are made up of all the different cultures with which they have contact. When two cultures or nations meet, ideas, language, and material goods are shared between them. That process of sharing forces them both to adapt and change. For this reason, there can be no "pure" Western or Eastern culture or nation. The act of creating a division creates an "Other" to engage with and to integrate (a process that denies it its identity).

Mimicry is the way in which a person or group adopts an idea from another culture—a term actually covering a range of potential strategies. It may be as simple as a direct attempt to copy or imitate that culture, but it can work in more complicated or ironic ways when a group uses another culture to reassert its own beliefs or ideas. This is a strategy of resistance, as mimicry turns into mockery. Adopting a different accent might be an attempt to present a higher social status (mimicry), or the voicing of things perceived to be ridiculous (mockery).

One example Bhabha gives of hybridity and mimicry is a tale of a group of Hindu* Indians (Hinduism is the largest religion in India) who are approached by an English missionary. At first, they refuse to accept that the Christian Bible could be true, because the missionary is not vegetarian (many Hindus avoid eating meat because they seek harmony with nature and practice a nonviolent lifestyle). The Bible has been translated into a local language, so becoming a hybrid text by combining its status as a core document of the West with the language and customs of the Indians. Crucially for Bhabha, both the Hindus and the missionaries are hybridized by this encounter. The missionaries are mimicking local beliefs to spread their message, but in doing so have to integrate local practices into their own beliefs; whereas the Hindus can use the hybrid text to gain social status within Indian society, because they have access to new knowledge created by the encounter.

The Location of Culture is now accepted as a seminal text in postcolonial thought and has gone through 13 editions since its publication. Bhabha continues to be an influential author in the field and his concepts have become standard in postcolonial theory and beyond.

Why Does The Location of Culture Matter?

The Location of Culture is one of the founding texts of postcolonial theory. Many of the concepts Bhabha puts forward in the work have been widely accepted. In particular, his concepts of mimicry and hybridity are now central to postcolonial theory. Most scholars working in that field today will have to respond to Bhabha's work at some level.

Alongside this theoretical innovation, *The Location of Culture* involves literary criticism. Bhabha uses culture, especially literature, as evidence for his thinking. In doing so, he shows the reader one way in which his theories might be applied to a range of literary texts, whether postcolonial or not. As a consequence, it is almost impossible to write about postcolonial literature without at least some knowledge of Bhabha's work.

Yet *The Location of Culture* is not only important to literature scholars. Bhabha's ideas have proved to be flexible and useful for many fields, with thinkers in disciplines as diverse as geography, the therapeutic and theoretical tools of psychoanalysis,* and physics also drawing upon them. His ideas have had an influence in architecture. Urban planners have adopted many of Bhabha's concepts and questions to help them consider how best to lay out a building, or even a whole city.

The Location of Culture is also an excellent model of problem-solving; students in any discipline trying to work out the practical applications of a theory will benefit from the text. Bhabha's style, dealing with the same questions from different points of view, shows how different approaches can be used together to solve a problem. Bhabha's ideas challenge us at a more fundamental level as well. *The Location of Culture* invites us to think about our identity as not fixed, but flexible. All identities are formed by the mixture of cultures, nations, and religious groupings. As a result, they can change, and we should be careful about adopting stereotypes or simple definitions. *The Location of Culture* shows us that many of the ideas we take for granted are actually politically charged, being used to construct and justify the world around us. Bhabha reminds his readers how important it is to challenge and question the "natural order" of things.

SECTION 1
INFLUENCES

THE AUTHOR AND THE HISTORICAL CONTEXT

KEY POINTS

- Homi K. Bhabha's *The Location of Culture* is one of the foundational texts of postcolonialism.*

- Though hard to quantify, Bhabha's experience of growing up in a minority community can perhaps be perceived in his work.

- Bhabha was significantly influenced by the theoretical developments of the 1970s and 1980s.

Why Read This Text?

Homi K. Bhabha's *The Location of Culture* (1994) is one of the foundational texts of the academic discipline of postcolonialism, a school of thought that offers a critical analysis of the social and cultural legacies of the colonial* period. Colonialism is the policy of claiming and exploiting "foreign" territories—an action that brings with it cultural, political, and social consequences for the colony's original inhabitants. Bhabha's book seeks, in a variety of ways, to challenge the classic narrative of the colonizer: the idea that the colonizers are somehow innately different from, and superior to, the original inhabitants of its colonies (commonly at a racial level). As such, colonization is defended by the colonizer as a benevolent enterprise of spreading "civilization." Primarily, this is undermined by Bhabha in his questioning of the basis of identity*; he continually challenges the notion of a stable sense of self (of either individuals or nations), suggesting instead that identity is

> ❝ I have lived that moment of the scattering of the people that in other times and other places, in the nations of others, becomes a time of gathering. ❞
>
> Homi K. Bhabha, *The Location of Culture*

"hybrid."* For Bhabha, this means that identity is created by being in between different cultures or ideologies. Importantly, colonizers and colonized alike are subject to hybridity, so that the experience of colonization changes them both.

The Location of Culture is in many ways a response to the Palestinian American scholar Edward Said,* whose 1978 book *Orientalism* is usually taken as being the text that inaugurated postcolonial studies as an academic discipline. In fact, Bhabha and Edward Said, alongside the Indian literary theorist Gayatri Spivak,* have been referred to as the "holy trinity" of postcolonial studies.[1] Most critics in the field deal with ideas generated by Bhabha, and so *The Location of Culture* is a useful source text. However, this is not to suggest it is a static text. Bhabha deliberately writes in a way that challenges set ideas, including his own, and so *The Location of Culture* has proved remarkably fertile as other critics have taken on and adapted Bhabha's thinking.

In the text, Bhabha introduced theoretical concepts that still underpin much of the work being done in postcolonial studies, and beyond. The concept of hybridity—that all identities are in some way a composite of different societies and experiences—is one of his most influential. As well as spurring much literary and social analysis of both colonized and colonizing cultures, the concept of hybridity has been adapted by theorists in fields as diverse as architecture, geography, and physics.

Author's Life

Bhabha was born in the city of Mumbai, India, in 1949. He attended private school and then took an undergraduate degree at the University of Mumbai. He did his postgraduate work at the University of Oxford.

Many commentators have seen Bhabha's insistence on the dislocation of culture (that is, his challenge to the automatic association of culture and territory) as a direct result of his own background. As a member of Mumbai's Parsi* minority, a group that maintains a degree of independent ethnic and cultural integrity from India's majority religious and cultural communities, Bhabha is intimately familiar with transnational or multicultural identities (identities forged across the boundaries of nation and culture). But Bhabha makes scant reference to such biographical influences in this or any of his other texts. Mostly, he insists that identity, in his own case and in that of the cultures he studies, "is never the affirmation of a pre-given identity, never a *self*-fulfilling prophecy."[2]

The influence of Bhabha's family and educational background on his intellectual output is difficult to quantify. In his insistence on the transnational characteristics of all cultures, it is at least possible to see some reflections on his own origin. Nevertheless, beyond all biographical details, Bhabha insists that subjectivity cannot be confined to characteristics considered "authentic" or "essential." For him, identity is always the product of an ongoing "performance" of selfhood.[3]

Similarly, we might suppose that Bhabha's educational background may seem to offer the possibility of "locating" the author and commenting on his intellectual influences (attending private school in India before studying at Oxford). But what he found at what he calls the "academic acme of ... literary culture"[4] actually inspired a new and determined concentration on writers and writings from the so-called margins that disturbed the self-confident Western discourse* about itself and about what it perceived to be "Other." ("Discourse" here refers to a system of language and assumptions that we draw on when we discuss something—in this case, the West and its colonies.) Bhabha remains at the center of Western academic culture in his role as Anne F. Rothenberg Professor of English and American Literature and Language at Harvard University.

Author's Background

It is not easy to trace the marks of the physical, social, and political environments that formed Bhabha in *The Location of Culture*. Indeed, disconnection from the "real world" in favor of total immersion in what the South African-born literary and cultural theorist Benita Parry* calls "The World according to The Word"[5] has been one of the most repeated criticisms of Bhabha. His insistence on the primacy of the text means we should be careful of mapping any contemporary events closely on to *The Location of Culture*. Similarly, the lengthy composition of the book (written over a decade) means that specific events become less important than theoretical development as a context for Bhabha's work. While growing up in India immediately after the nation's independence from Britain influenced his interests in questions of nationhood and identity, the most obvious spark for Bhabha's writing was the development of poststructuralist* thought during the 1970s and 1980s, as he began writing the series of essays that would make up *The Location of Culture*. (Poststructuralism is an approach to the analysis of culture that holds that, since knowledge itself is a social construct, we cannot lay claim to the possibility of any "objective" truth.)

Accusations of academic isolation are, however, at least partly challenged by Bhabha's employment resumé; he has been chair of the Global Agenda Council on Human Equality of the World Economic Forum* and a trustee of the *World Report on Cultural*

Diversity by the United Nations body UNESCO.* Besides his contribution to these institutions of international stature, in 1999 he was cited as one of the journal *Newsweek*'s "100 Americans for the next century" and has collaborated with novelists, poets, and sculptors from across the globe.

NOTES

1   Robert J. C. Young, *Colonial Desire: Hybridity in Theory, Culture, and Race* (London: Routledge, 1995), 154.

2   Homi K. Bhabha, *The Location of Culture* (Abingdon: Routledge Classics, 2004), 64.

3   Bhabha, *Location of Culture*, 209.

4   Bhabha, *Location of Culture*, xi.

5   Benita Parry, "Signs of Our Times: Discussion of Homi K. Bhabha's *The Location of Culture,*" *Third Text* 28/29 (1994): 9.

MODULE 2
ACADEMIC CONTEXT

KEY POINTS

- Postcolonialism* is the study of the ideas and legacies of colonial* rule, on both the colonizer and colonized.
- Postcolonial theorists are interested in how individuals are constructed and represented by the colonial power to which they are subject.
- Bhabha challenged the idea that there was a simple binary between colonizer and colonized.

The Work in its Context

Homi K. Bhabha's *The Location of Culture* is one of the seminal texts of postcolonialism: the study of the cultures that have moved beyond colonial rule to independence, often with the reassertion of their national identity,* and of the legacies of imperial rule on the culture and society of the postcolonial nation. It discusses reflections on the strategies and discourses* generated by colonialism.

In many ways, postcolonialism is in fact a successor to earlier intellectual movements that had similarly challenged the categorization of nations and peoples on a spectrum between civility and savagery. One of the justifications for colonialism was the idea that "more developed" or "civilized" nations were duty-bound to rule over nations of cultures that were seen as less developed, or savage, in order to help them develop. The first landmark text in the field of postcolonial studies was Edward Said's* *Orientalism* (1978), which argued that Western (or Occidental) artists, writers, and colonial administrators had constructed a distorted image of the East (or Orient) based not on observable facts but on preconceived notions

> ❝ Can the subaltern speak? What must the elite do to watch out for the continuing construction of the subaltern? The question of 'woman' seems most problematic in this context. Clearly, if you are poor, black and female you get it in three ways. ❞
> Gayatri Chakravorty Spivak, "Can the Subaltern Speak?"

about a fundamentally exotic and alien "Other."* The process of "Othering" required a division of the world into Western and not-Western. This was extremely prejudicial, because the category not-Western came to mean barbarous, uncivilized, lazy, or savage (in contrast to the civilized, industrious West). Later thinkers, such as the literary theorist Gayatri Chakravorty Spivak,* built on Said's work, but showed that his theory of Orientalism did not apply equally across peoples and times.

Despite the increasing visibility of postcolonialism thinking throughout the 1980s and 1990s, the principal concepts in this emerging discipline were constantly changing. For Bhabha, this was not a weakness, and in *The Location of Culture* he suggests that postcolonial thought must embrace constant changeability. He argued that, unlike intellectual movements such as Marxism* (the analytical approach and political philosophy based on the thought of the German economist and political theorist Karl Marx), it had no master narrative from which all subsequent analysis necessarily emerged.[1] For Bhabha, postcolonial studies were based on the erosion of clear boundaries in all spheres and it could not abandon that legacy for the sake of stable, dependable theoretical positions and constancy in its statements.

Overview of the Field
Together with Said and Spivak, Bhabha is one of the cofounders of postcolonialism. Although they analyze many similar themes

(particularly subaltern* interpretations and narrations of colonial and postcolonial history—that is, the interpretations and narrations of those of low status whose voices are routinely excluded from cultural analysis and the historical record), mutual references between Bhabha and Spivak are surprisingly few. Spivak is perhaps the best-known member of the Subaltern Studies Group,* along with its founder Ranajit Guha.* Her work, and that of the group, focuses on recovering the voices at the very edge of colonialism—such as women or minority ethnic and sexual groups—who might otherwise be ignored in mainstream histories of colonization. Spivak's work therefore focuses on the marginal "men and women among the illiterate peasantry, the tribals, the lowest strata,"[2] in order to uncover the full social effects of colonialism.

Nevertheless, despite the obvious similarities between Said, Bhabha, and Spivak, care must be taken when thinking of postcolonialism as a wholly coherent "intellectual school." For Bhabha, the impetus is constant experimentation, or what he calls the "moment of primary elaboration,"[3] in which students of postcolonialism consistently transform its foundational ideas.

In this respect, the essays in *The Location of Culture* can be read as a response to the influential psychiatrist and cultural theorist Frantz Fanon's* *Black Skin, White Masks* (1952) and Said's *Orientalism*. The former explores the divided self-perception of the colonizers and their colonial subjects, suggesting that both identities come together in a "zone of occult instability."[4] The latter is credited with first applying poststructuralist* thought to the subject of colonialism, and thereby inaugurating the academic discipline within which Bhabha was to become so prominent: postcolonialism.

Academic Influences

The Location of Culture engages in critical dialogue with Said's text. Bhabha goes beyond a simple analysis of European attitudes towards the Oriental "Other" to argue that the coherent Western identity upon which these assumptions and prejudices were based was actually undermined by contradictions, fears, and a profound ambiguity that made the very idea of identity problematic.

Though Bhabha draws on a wide variety of critical thinkers, the most important for the lines of inquiry pursued in the book are the ideas and works of poststructuralists such as the French philosopher and social theorist Michel Foucault* and the French philosopher Jacques Derrida.* From these thinkers, Bhabha inherited a stubborn suspicion of "the order of things" as presented by the philosophical tradition that came to prominence with the Enlightenment* (an intellectual current of eighteenth-century Europe) anchored in scientific investigation, deductive reason, and the rule of law.

Like Foucault and Derrida, Bhabha saw apparently universal and value-free methods of ordering and comprehending the world as ideologically charged discourses within which partial knowledge was linked to a desire for total power. In other words, the Western philosophic tradition claimed to have the key to comprehending all the world's mysteries, and therefore claimed the right to rule over that categorized world and everyone in it. Bhabha's work challenged the primacy of such discourses.

Bhabha also combined the intellectual tradition of Foucault and Derrida with some of the psychoanalytic* insights of Sigmund Freud,* the founder of the psychoanalytic tradition, and of Jacques Lacan,* a psychoanalyst who made an important contribution to poststructuralist theory. In essence, he questioned the alleged integrity of Western thought and identity. Rather than seeing this as a total or complete system, Bhabha revealed the anxieties and repressed desires that disturbed the whole notion of order and progress, both in colonial and colonized countries.

NOTES

1   Homi K. Bhabha, *The Location of Culture* (Abingdon: Routledge Classics, 2004), 9.

2   Gayatri Chakravorty Spivak, "Can the Subaltern Speak?" in *Marxism and the Interpretation of Culture*, ed. Cary Nelson and Lawrence Grossberg (Urbana: University of Illinois Press, 1988), 271–313 (278).

3   Fawzia Afzal-Khan, "Surviving Theory: A Conversation with Homi K. Bhabha," in *The Pre-Occupation of Postcolonial Studies*, ed. Fawzia Afzal-Khan and Kalpana Seshadri-Crooks (Durham, NC: Duke University Press, 2000), 372.

4   Frantz Fanon, *The Wretched of the Earth* (New York: Grove Press, 1961), cited in Homi K. Bhabha, *The Location of Culture* (Abingdon: Routledge, 2011), 218.

MODULE 3
THE PROBLEM

KEY POINTS

- *The Location of Culture* challenges the idea of a stable identity of either colonized or colonizers.
- Bhabha helped to develop postcolonial* theory by showing the wide range of strategies of resistance to colonialism.*
- Bhabha's work combined existing theories in a way that challenged them, and produced new readings of the cultural history of colonization.

Core Question

In *The Location of Culture*, Homi K. Bhabha questions the coherence of the ideas and discourses* of European colonialism that had developed from the eighteenth century onwards. He challenges the philosophical foundations underpinning the Western world view (such as the notions of reason, order, progress, and a self-affirming distinction between the civilization of Europe and the barbarity of the "Other"* or "the Rest"). Instead of a single, "civilized" identity,* Bhabha shows that colonizers have traces of many "Others" in them, which undermines their claim to purity and superiority. In doing so, *The Location of Culture* provides a powerful statement on behalf of postcolonialism. By fracturing the ideologies of the colonizers, Bhabha attempts to realign Western culture around the postcolonial, rather than colonial, project.

This key question—how coherent is European colonialism?—leads to others of equal importance. What implications would instabilities and ambiguities within the discourse of colonialism have for the self-confident identity of the colonizers and the

> 66 To speak of Orientalism therefore is to speak mainly, though not exclusively, of a British and French colonial enterprise, a project whose dimensions take in such disparate realms as the imagination itself, the whole of India and the Levant, the biblical texts and the biblical lands, the spice trade, colonial armies and a long tradition of colonial administrators, a formidable scholarly corpus, innumerable Oriental "experts" and "hands," an Oriental professorate, a complex array of "Oriental" ideas (Oriental despotism, Oriental splendor, cruelty, sensuality), many Eastern sects, philosophies and wisdoms domesticated for local European use. 99
>
> Edward Said, *Orientalism*

subjugated identities of the colonized? What implications would recognition of these ambiguities have for contemporary perceptions of modern developed nations (whose history is so inextricably interlinked with colonialism)? These questions are important both for the interpretation of colonial history and for contemporary understandings of concepts such as "development" or "progress."

In the series of essays that make up *The Location of Culture*, Bhabha approaches his core question from a variety of theoretical standpoints, using a wide range of literary material produced from within colonial and postcolonial cultures. Though these are not "coherent," in the sense that they do not carefully build up a single thesis, the fragmentary nature of the essay collection is actually the perfect vehicle for Bhabha's arguments about the multifaceted identity of postcolonial subjects.

The Participants

The Location of Culture can be seen as a natural outcome of earlier developments in politics, critical theory (the analysis of culture, society, knowledge, and factors such as the role of language in the formation of meaning), and the therapeutic method of psychoanalysis.* A genealogy of postcolonial thought would include those who resisted colonialism, particularly those who did so in print, since for Bhabha the "discovery of the English book" is a master narrative of "colonial authority and a signifier of colonial desire and discipline."[1] In this category we would find pamphlets such as the Indian political leader Mahatma Gandhi's* 1909 *Hind Swaraj* (Indian Home Rule), or the Indianized Bible demanded by the nineteenth-century natives of India, documents that are "using the powers of hybridity* to resist"[2] the colonizers (that is, they adopted some of the colonizer's strategies in order to defeat or resist colonialism).

Bhabha, though, adds nuance to the idea of resistance in this fashion. He did not subscribe to what he called Frantz Fanon's* "state of emergency" type of writing, which turned from consideration of the "psychic projections in the pathological colonial relation"[3] (the psychologically damaging nature of the relation between colonizer and colonized) to a call for armed resistance against colonization. Instead, he aimed to demonstrate that the most meaningful resistance would emerge not from fighting, but from a committed exploration of the ideological contradictions of colonialism: "It is from that tension—both psychic and political—that a strategy of subversion emerges."[4] In opposition to Edward Said,* Bhabha aimed to challenge the alleged omnipotence of colonial discourse against which colonized subjects were powerless, observing instead the potential for active resistance in the liminal* ("in between") space between representation and reality.

The book's combination of ideas from psychoanalysis and poststructuralism* pushes Bhabha further than many of his predecessors and contemporaries, and produces critical concepts that have become indispensable in many disciplines such as cultural hybridity,* mimicry,* and the Third Space* (a term used in the social sciences to describe a space that exists alongside the public and private spheres, demonstrating characteristics of both).

The Contemporary Debate

It is important to remember that Bhabha's *The Location of Culture* is an anthology of essays produced over a decade. Ten of the 12 essays had been previously published in academic journals or books and their content had changed very little between their first publication and their publication in the book. It is therefore necessary to consider the changing "intellectual battlefield" between the appearance of the individual essays during the 1980s and the book's publication in 1994.

In 1985, when the first essay was published, the emergence of postcolonialism as a discipline (the publication of Edward Said's *Orientalism* in 1978 is generally taken to be its genesis) was incomplete. Objections existed not just to the ideas put forward by postcolonial scholars, but to their very existence as a distinct school of thought. As the 1980s progressed, these initial dismissals were replaced by more substantial engagement with the theoretical tenets of the emerging discipline. Perhaps the most important transformation was brought about by the work of Bhabha himself, and in particular by his critical engagement with *Orientalism*.

Although celebrating many of Said's insights, Bhabha also perceived shortcomings in *Orientalism*. First, he critiques Said for presenting colonial discourse as a one-way monologue between the colonizers and the colonized. Bhabha reinstated colonized people as actors in their own identity and destiny, capable of responding to, and so disturbing, colonial discourse.

Second, Bhabha suggests that although Said referred to

the inherent ambivalence of colonial discourse, meaning its inconsistency and contradictions, he paid "inadequate attention to representation as a concept."[5] Bhabha argues, in effect, that Said's formulation of Orientalism only conceives of the colonized–colonizer relationship as a symmetrical relationship of binaries such as self–other, or master–slave that can only be escaped by inverting that relationship. Bhabha fundamentally reappraises the possibilities for local resistance to colonialism by exposing the disturbing effects of stereotypes, the endless mixings of hybridity, and the mockery at the heart of mimicry.

NOTES

1   Homi K. Bhabha, *The Location of Culture* (Abingdon: Routledge Classics, 2004), 102.

2   Bhabha, *Location of Culture*, 118.

3   Homi K. Bhabha, "Foreword: Remembering Fanon—Self, Psyche and the Colonial Condition," in Frantz Fanon, *Black Skin, White Masks* (London: Pluto Press, 1986), xxiii.

4   Bhabha, "Foreword: Remembering Fanon," xxiii.

5   Bhabha, *Location of Culture*, 72.

MODULE 4
THE AUTHOR'S CONTRIBUTION

KEY POINTS

- Bhabha aims to reveal the instabilities in colonial* discourse.*

- He challenges existing ideas of the colonized–colonizer relationship, to show how forms of direct and indirect resistance could be articulated.

- Though few of Bhabha's ideas were generated by him, his originality came in the combination and application of theories from other disciplines.

Author's Aims

Homi K. Bhabha's main aim in the essays that make up *The Location of Culture* is to challenge fundamental tenets of Western ontology* (the philosophical study of being and existence).

Bhabha sought to question the ways in which categories of people (such as West/East, civilized/barbarian) were created and perpetuated. In particular, he wanted to show that the use of these categories in colonial thought relied on the fact they were oppositional—and that their opposition brought them into a closer, more intertwined relationship than had previously been realized. In doing so, Bhabha aimed to destabilize apparently stable markers of identity,* such as nationality, gender, and class, and to think about them as the "sites of collaboration and contestation"[1] that make up an unstable, hybrid* self or society. In effect, he wanted to show that there was no such thing as a pure or essential self; instead, all identities are composites of the many different cultures and beliefs with which they interact.

> **❝** Bhabha's aim is to put the skids under every cherished doctrine of Western Enlightenment, from the idea of progress to the unity of the self, from the classical work of art to the notions of law and civility. **❞**
>
> Terry Eagleton, "Goodbye to the Enlightenment," *Guardian*

Because *The Location of Culture* is a curated collection of essays, care must be taken when searching for an overall coherence between, or even within, the essays. Whereas other writers patiently build their arguments through example and counterexample, Bhabha's work displays the same kind of expansive "disorder" he observes in colonial texts. It is playful, and often returns to the same concept from a new angle, developing or challenging it. In this way, the overall aim of challenging fixed identities disrupts even the identity of *The Location of Culture* itself.

Approach

While many, if not all, of the theoretical concepts in *The Location of Culture* were first proposed by other thinkers, Bhabha would probably object to the notion of wholly original thought, suggesting instead that there is great potential for innovation in the reiteration of existing ideas, where each new articulation leads to subtle adaptations. As an example, in chapter 10 he tells the story of chapatis (unleavened flatbread) that allegedly circulated among the conspirators during the Indian Mutiny* (a series of military and civilian uprisings against British colonial rule in northern India in 1857–8). Whether the story is true or not, its reiteration as rumor and hearsay, or what Bhabha calls "its *circulation* and *contagion*," caused near panic among the colonial authorities because the precise meaning of the chapatis could never be determined; each telling of the story came with a slightly different understanding of the event. In the same way, Bhabha's work continually returns to core ideas or theories, but each time demonstrates a new way of thinking about them, or applying them to different texts and times.

Bhabha thus seeks to undermine the logic of academic discourse and upset the neat order of dialectical* argument (argument in which opposite positions are finally resolved in a synthesis). Bhabha is attempting to show that colonial discourse, which claims to be coherent and inevitable, is actually unstable and fragmented. His writing reflects this argument by refusing any final or definitive interpretation of his ideas. Instead, he asks his reader to look upon the text as an ongoing process of sharing and questioning ideas.

Contribution in Context

Many of Bhabha's key ideas are developments from thinkers in other fields than postcolonialism. Most notably, the notion of cultural hybridity was common to anthropologists (scholars of human culture, belief, and society) long before Bhabha adopted and adapted it. Particularly close is the Cuban anthropologist Fernando Ortiz Fernandez's* "transculturation," a term coined to describe the interactions and negotiations he observed when two cultures come into contact, and explain the complex cultural fusions that made all claims to authentic or "pure" Latin American identities difficult to sustain.

Finally, Bhabha's thoughts on agency* (the capacity to act according to a decision) can be traced to the French philosophers Michel Foucault* and Jacques Derrida.* For the former, the authorities had instigated methods to block and invalidate sexual expression and, thus, unwittingly stimulated the kind of subtle but potent resistance Bhabha sees in colonial history. For the latter, the uncertainty inherent in all languages made them vulnerable to the resistance that would flourish in the gap between sign (simply, anything that conveys *meaning*) and signifier (a sign's physical form—a sound, printed word, or image). For Bhabha, this was particularly acute in the language of colonial authority, which presents itself as being "the representation of an essence"—that is, a universal, unchallengeable whole. Bhabha shows how, because they rely on a binary of opposition to the colonized "Other," the ideas of colonization can only ever be a "partial presence" in the identity of either colonizer or colonized.[2]

NOTES

1   Homi K. Bhabha, *The Location of Culture* (Abingdon: Routledge Classics, 2004), 2.

2   Bhabha, *Location of Culture,* 123.

SECTION 2
IDEAS

MAIN IDEAS

KEY POINTS

- Bhabha is interested in the construction of individual and collective identity,* as well as the role of theory in resisting colonialism.*
- Bhabha argues that all identities (individual or national) are fragmented, hybrid,* and unstable.
- Bhabha's argument relies on the continued reiteration, alteration, and questioning of his central ideas.

Key Themes

Central to Homi K. Bhabha's *The Location of Culture* is the idea that the identities of colonizers and colonized (whether individuals or a society) are inherently unstable, fractured, and hybrid. That is, there is no "pure" identity, since all identities are formed by the presence of traces of different cultures within the subject. Naturally, this leads to a consideration of nationality and nationhood, which Bhabha sees as much more fractured and hybrid than a standard definition would allow. As well as this hybrid identity, Bhabha discusses the role of theory as a mechanism of colonial resistance, in contrast to direct action.

The key themes of Bhabha's work are:

- Theory is resistance.
- Colonized people have agency* through language.
- Identities are hybrid.
- The idea of "nationhood" or "nationality" is not fixed by, or reliant on, borders.

> **❝** Hybridity intervenes in the exercise of authority not merely to indicate the impossibility of its identity but to represent the unpredictability of its presence. **❞**
>
> Homi K. Bhabha, *The Location of Culture*

Bhabha orders and interrelates his key themes through a repetition that involves subtle alterations in emphasis, tone, and theoretical approach. In many ways, he approaches the notion of ordering ideas logically with suspicion, since he wants to challenge and engage his reader, not present a fixed set of ideas. So while it is possible to extract his principal themes and to organize them into a systematic list, a close reading of the text will constantly upset any sense of order, as ideas seem to retreat from, rather than move toward, definition and conclusion.

Exploring the Ideas

Chapters 1 and 2 of *The Location of Culture* are an appropriate introduction because they emphasize the fundamental importance of theory within Bhabha's intellectual project. He argues that "theory" is not just a tool for abstract study but an essential prerequisite to social, political, and cultural activism—what he calls "a productive matrix that defines the 'social' and makes it available as an objective of and for, action."[1] For Bhabha, the act of writing and reading reveals that dominant ideologies are not natural or unquestionable, and so is even more important as an act of resistance than direct action. His work, and the work of other theorists, provides the terminology and understanding needed to resist dominant narratives such as colonization.

A related theme is the question of agency: to what degree were colonized people able to resist the overbearing authority of colonial discourse★ and practice? One of Bhabha's central arguments is that the "ambivalence"★ (meaning inconsistencies and contradictions) of both discourse and practice opened up spaces (often referred to as liminal★—"in between"—spaces, or the Third Space★) for textual (rather than military) resistance. In chapter 4, for example, he argues that mimicry★ could actually be infused with farce to become a mockery of colonial culture. Doing so is resistance, because the language upon which colonialism relies (for attitudes such as notions of superiority, for example) is undermined—in effect, it is hard to appear powerful when your ideas or culture are subject to mockery.

The hybridity of identity is the third key theme of the book. Bhabha illustrates this idea with reference to the Martinique-born theorist Frantz Fanon's★ *Black Skin, White Masks* and an exploration of what Bhabha sees as the fundamental ambivalence of supposedly stable and coherent colonial discourses and identities. For him, these matters open spaces for local resistance to colonial authority. He presents his understanding of nation and nationhood as a combination of established traditions and constantly creative performance. He goes on to discuss the cultural hybridity evident in many colonial and postcolonial★ texts, suggesting that exploring the contradictions within the textual narratives or depictions can act as a tool for resistance against the misrepresentation of colonized peoples.

The fourth key theme concerns nation and nationhood. Bhabha challenges any face-value understandings of these terms. He suggests instead that they arise from a tense interplay between two types of nationhood. The first type is what is taught about nations' established traditions, which he calls the "linear narrative of the nation" or *pedagogical* (that is, educational) nationhood.[2] This is, in effect, the classic narrative of the development of a nation from its founding to the present day, a narrative that Bhabha argues serves primarily to legitimize the nation itself, making its people secondary. Against this, he places the second type of nationhood, which he calls *performative* nationhood. This is derived from the acts of its subjects (or citizens), and the varied ways in which they show, embrace, or challenge the central idea of nationality or nationhood. For Bhabha, performative nationhood involves the constant reinterpretation of any sense of national community. This results in the erosion of supposed unambiguous borders around nations and their peoples, opening them up to the "Otherness"★ that has always been internally present.

Language and Expression

Bhabha's approach to theory and his unusual writing style was a practical application of his insights. In a later piece he argued that it is necessary, when reading *The Location of Culture*, "to appreciate its metaphoric structure—the terms in which it may not be quite what it claims it is and why it may be something other than it knows itself to be."[3] *The Location of Culture* actively deploys the ideas of hybridity and mimicry that it discusses. That is, the form of writing Bhabha uses is itself a strategy to challenge the smooth transmission of a single or simple idea. By returning to ideas from new angles or theoretical standpoints, Bhabha encourages the reader to take nothing as settled, even *The Location of Culture* itself.

Some consolation may be drawn from the fact that Bhabha himself recognizes that his meaning is often elusive, and sees this as a key element of the activity of reading. "The reader, for me," he says, "must feel engaged at all levels of witnessing, in the very midst of unfolding of a theoretical idea."[4] That is, Bhabha demands that his readers do not just passively take in what has been written, but see themselves as being in conversation with the text. Rather than simply attempting to persuade, Bhabha wants to show the many ways in which an idea might unfold, encouraging his readers to extend or recombine his ideas in new ways.

NOTES

1   Homi K. Bhabha, *The Location of Culture* (Abingdon: Routledge Classics, 2004), 34.

2   Bhabha, *Location of Culture*, 142.

3   Fawzia Afzal-Khan, "Surviving Theory: A Conversation with Homi K. Bhabha," in *The Pre-Occupation of Postcolonial Studies*, ed. Fawzia Afzal-Khan and Kalpana Seshadri-Crooks (Durham, NC: Duke University Press, 2000), 371.

4   Afzal-Khan, "Surviving Theory," 371.

MODULE 6
SECONDARY IDEAS

KEY POINTS

- Bhabha has many secondary ideas, but two that are significant are the production of "uncanny"* effects by colonization,* and its stereotyping of itself and the "Other."*

- The uncanny fractures the sense of colonial identity* by revealing the (often brutal) oppression on which its civilization is built.

- The discussion of stereotyping helps to justify the postcolonial* project, since many colonial stereotypes still persist, in modified forms, in Western culture.

Other Ideas

The separation of Homi K. Bhabha's thought in *The Location of Culture* into superior and subordinate ideas is problematic. Bhabha largely turns away from any dialectical* development of his thesis towards a definitive conclusion, and instead approaches his central themes from several complementary perspectives. Within *The Location of Culture* none of these perspectives are given precedence over others, so the text itself resists categorization into major and minor ideas. This module will focus on two that are arguably more peripheral, because the central concepts could, if necessary, be understood without them: the uncanny and stereotypes.

"The uncanny" is a term coined by the founding psychoanalyst Sigmund Freud* to designate the intrusion of something unusual into the normal, so that it is familiar but disturbing. One example might be the way that mannequins or robots are "dead" things that can sometimes look or seem alive. For Bhabha, colonialism produces

> **❝** An uncanny experience occurs either when repressed infantile complexes have been revived by some impression, or when the primitive beliefs we have surmounted seem once more to be confirmed. **❞**
>
> Sigmund Freud, "The Uncanny"

uncanniness because it is built on cultural or physical violence while styling itself as civilized and ordered. Stereotypes are what allow this apparent paradox, because they are the way in which the dualities (order/disorder, civilized/savage) that justify colonization are constructed.

For Freud, identity was haunted by primitive, unfinished or traumatic events and experiences from the past, always threatening to irrupt "uncannily" into the present and disturb our sense of selves. Bhabha uses the notion of the uncanny as part of his overarching project to examine the West, and the sum of personal identities that compose it as a patient whose mental malaise requires diagnosis and cure.

Bhabha argues that stereotypes emerged in colonial discourse* because of the unavoidable fact that colonial domination was not a "natural" occurrence; it required an ideological structure to justify it. This was provided by the stereotypical representation (in, for example, literature or art) of the colonized subject as inherently inferior, lazy, and stupid: "as a population of degenerate types on the basis of racial origin."[1]

These two concepts help to build on, and more fully explain, the central theme of hybridity* within *The Location of Culture*. Bhabha's text is a sustained and coherent assault on the modern West's self-satisfaction with its seemingly uninterrupted progress towards civility, equality, and justice—an intellectual model produced by the period of European intellectual history known as the Enlightenment.* By using the concept of the uncanny to reveal the ways in which modernity is haunted by its colonial past, because its progress and civility rely on often brutal colonization, Bhabha makes this self-satisfaction unsustainable. Secondly, and more specifically, his suggestion that attitudes and practices prevalent during colonization (and in literature of the period) remain relevant for modern-day self-perceptions and projections helps to justify his overall project and methodology.

Exploring the Ideas

Bhabha does not simply challenge the accuracy of stereotypes or propose a more authentic counter-identity. Instead, he seeks to demonstrate that such representations (like the discourse from which they emerged) were fundamentally ambivalent* because of two critical factors. First, colonial authorities actually recognized stereotypes for what they were: a means by which to "justify conquest and to establish systems of administration and instruction."[2] Second, the insistence on the inherent and irreversible "backwardness" of colonized peoples, rendering them suitable only for subjugation, actually contradicts the civilizing mission that, in Bhabha's words, "provides the manifest justification for the project of colonization."[3] In this way, the whole notion of stereotypes becomes unstable and, in turn, destabilizes the colonial project that relies upon them for its authority.

In his readings of colonial literature, Bhabha uses the uncanny to unsettle modernity's self-confidence in its own "superior" civility by pointing to the presence of savage colonialism at its very genesis. By bringing this uncomfortable past back into present consciousness, Bhabha not only criticizes attitudes prevalent during colonialism, but also challenges modern-day Western societies to look again at the foundations of their sense of identity. For Bhabha, the fact that texts which portray colonial stereotypes, such as those by the novelists Joseph Conrad* and E. M. Forster,* are still part of the Western canon* (the body of literature considered representative of the Western literary tradition, and worthy of special consideration) has as much to say about the Western present as it does about its past.

Overlooked

The Location of Culture has become canonical in postcolonial theory, and an important text in several other disciplines such as geography and architecture; it has been rigorously dissected, analyzed, and criticized for nearly 20 years. As such, there are no elements of the text that have been obviously neglected or wholly overlooked. It could be argued that critical readers have even uncovered facets and applications that the author himself may not have anticipated, such as the way in which the Third Space,* which for Bhabha is the imaginary frontier at which two cultures meet, is used in geography and education.

The political geographer Edward Soja* (a scholar of the ways in which people in different parts of the world have organized themselves politically) has developed Bhabha's concept of the Third Space, moving beyond the duality between space as material and space as a concept. Soja uses the term "Third Space" to try to imagine the ways in which real and imaginary spaces intersect. For example, a garden might be simultaneously a simple garden and also a way of thinking metaphorically about the layout of a district, city or even country.[4]

In education, theorists such as Kris D. Gutierrez* have used the concept of the Third Space to think about the interaction between a child's home, social life, and school life. They consider "what it means to learn in familiar, new, and overlapping contexts, in rapidly shifting practices and communities."[5] Doing so requires breaking the boundaries between home and school, and seeing the school as a Third Space, a point that combines the total lived experience of the child. Only by teaching in this way, Gutierrez argues, can the full development of the child be attended to.

NOTES

1   Homi K. Bhabha, *The Location of Culture* (Abingdon: Routledge Classics, 2004), 101.

2   Bhabha, *Location of Culture*, 101.

3   Bhabha, *Location of Culture*, 111.

4   Edward W. Soja, *Thirdspace: Journeys to Los Angeles and Other Real-and-Imagined Places* (Oxford: Blackwell, 1996).

5   K. D. Gutiérrez, "Developing a Sociocritical Literacy in the Third Space," *Reading Research Quarterly* 43, no. 2 (2008), 148–64 (150).

ACHIEVEMENT

KEY POINTS

- *The Location of Culture* is widely regarded as one of the most seminal texts in the field of postcolonial* studies.
- Bhabha's text updated the work of the founders of postcolonialism by introducing new theoretical developments from other fields.
- Although global politics during the 1990s seemed to limit the impact of Bhabha's work, recent events have given it fresh relevance.

Assessing the Argument

The Location of Culture remains one of Homi K. Bhabha's most influential texts. Alongside the work of the Edward Said* and Gayatri Spivak,* the book is one of the most important texts in postcolonial thought.

Bhabha's arguments were developed over many years, in different occasional pieces, before being collected in *The Location of Culture*. Additional material added to the volume, especially the introduction, helps Bhabha draw together the threads of his thought and establish that "the cultural and historical hybridity* of the postcolonial world is taken as the paradigmatic place of departure."[1] (A "paradigm" is an intellectual framework inside which evidence or theory is interpreted and understood.)

The arguments that Bhabha is making throughout the book have become widely accepted, even commonplace, among postcolonial theorists and thinkers. Bhabha's self-assessment of them as a "paradigmatic place of departure" is apt, for they are

> ❝ Bhabha's influence on the field of postcolonial theory cannot be overestimated, despite often vehement criticism of his postmodern, elitist stance as a Third World intellectual. ❞
>
> Martina Ghosh-Schellhorn, "Spaced In-Between"

now so fundamental that other research, even arguably the whole discipline of postcolonial studies, has been built upon them.

There is no question, then, that Bhabha achieved his aims in creating a theoretical system with which to challenge dominant narratives: "hybridity—and its related notions of third space and the in-between—has gained considerable currency as a counter-language to the constructedness of national identity* associated with colonial settings."[2] The creation of this "counter-language" is the core achievement of *The Location of Culture*.

Achievement in Context

Given the chronology of the essays in the anthology, *The Location of Culture* can be read as a contribution to the so-called "culture wars" of the 1980s and 1990s that saw a rise in "political and social hostility rooted in different systems of moral understanding."[3] These two systems can be broadly defined as orthodox (conservative) and progressive (liberal). Those decades saw often ferocious debates about culture and identity across a whole range of issues such as sexuality, abortion, patriotism, and even education, which continue today. Bhabha's key contribution was to destabilize both terms and establish the intellectual tradition of "interrogating 'identity' rather than asserting its inviolability."[4] In other words, he offered a critique of "identity" that challenges our understanding of it as a constant, secure phenomenon.

By the end of the twentieth century, critics of *The Location of Culture* claimed that Bhabha's formulations were no longer relevant. In *Empire* (2000), Michael Hardt and Antonio Negri described a globalized and technologically interconnected world that had "absorbed the lessons of mobility, indeterminacy, and hybridity" that postcolonialism had made so much of.[5] They claimed that Bhabha's insistence on the ambivalence of supposedly rigid binaries between colonizer and colonized, core and margin, civilization and barbarity was "entirely insufficient for theorizing contemporary global power."[6]

However, the terrorist attacks of September 11, 2001 in New York and Washington seemed to demonstrate the ongoing relevance of *The Location of Culture* as the West reacted to 9/11* by defaulting to binary explanations (West–East) and insisting once again on the allegedly eternal and irredeemable differences between "the World of Order and the World of Disorder."[7] Bhabha's questioning of such binaries in the discourse* and practices of nineteenth-century colonialism* was in many ways revitalized. The fundamental flaws of stereotypes, the uncanny* disorder that upsets modernity's self-confident civilization when "barbarity" is revealed as the foundation of "civilization," and the hybridity at the core of all "essential" identities came to prominence in public debate once more. "The aftermath of 9/11," Bhabha insisted in 2003, "has made even more urgent the '80s endeavor to think of issues relating to political and cultural difference beyond the polarities of power and identity."[8]

Limitations

Some critics have questioned the universality of the theories used by Bhabha to develop his core ideas. The British scholar and political campaigner Bart Moore-Gilbert,* for example, has argued that the psychoanalysis* at the heart of Bhabha's analysis was conceived in the West and displayed a fundamentally North

American and Eurocentric world view (that is, a world view founded on the primacy of Western perspectives and assumptions) that could only be awkwardly applied elsewhere. Similarly, the philosophical position on which so much of his intellectual project relies—that of poststructuralism*—is European in origin and, frequently, practice. Bhabha's work, then, risks itself becoming in between; in trying to bring together European thought and Asian (colonial) experience, it risks belonging to neither category.

There are also implications for Bhabha's theory in global political events. After the end of the decades-long period of global tension between nations aligned to the United States and those aligned to the Soviet Union known as the Cold War,* the 1990s saw the apparent triumph of liberal* capitalist* democracy—the political and economic system dominant in the West today. In the words of the political scientist Francis Fukuyama,* whose influential essay "The End of History" sums up the newfound security and confidence of the West, the defeat of communism* heralded the "total exhaustion of viable systematic alternatives to Western liberalism."[9] If, as Fukuyama suggests, there is now only one system to belong to across the globe, then Bhabha's work on the interplay between different cultures, or even between the global and local, will become irrelevant, since there will be no cultures to be "between."

NOTES

1   Homi K. Bhabha, *The Location of Culture* (Abingdon: Routledge Classics, 2004), 21.

2   Sarah Maitland, "'In-Between' a Rock and a 'Third Space'? On the Trouble with Ambivalent Metaphors of Translation," *Translation Studies,* 2015, 1–9 (1), accessed November 15, 2015, doi: 10.1080/14781700.2015.1085432.

3   James Davison Hunter, *Culture Wars: The Struggle to Define America* (New York: Basic Books, 1991), 42.

4   Homi K. Bhabha, "Making Difference: Homi K. Bhabha on the Legacy of the Culture Wars," *Artforum* 46, no. 8 (2003): 75.

5   Michael Hardt and Antonio Negri, *Empire* (Cambridge, MA: Harvard University Press, 2000), 76.

6   Hardt and Negri, *Empire*, 146.

7   Thomas Friedman, op-ed in *New York Times*, February 16, 2003, cited in Bhabha, "Making Difference," 234.

8   Bhabha, "Making Difference," 234.

9   Francis Fukuyama, "The End of History," *The National Interest* (1989), 3–18 (3).

MODULE 8
PLACE IN THE AUTHOR'S WORK

KEY POINTS

- Bhabha has consistently questioned the nature of colonial* and postcolonial* identity*.

- *The Location of Culture* is a mid-career reflection on his work to date, and an attempt to (loosely) establish themes and continuities within it.

- The book established Bhabha's reputation as a leading theorist of postcolonial studies.

Positioning

A current reading could place Homi K. Bhabha's *The Location of Culture* at an important mid-point of his career, in that it distils his work up to 1994 and also indicates the ongoing direction of his themes and theories. The book is supplemented by a lengthy introduction and the inclusion of two previously unpublished essays that help to unify his work to that point, and allow Bhabha to reflect on "the join"—the centralizing thread of his work that he sees as the study of "those who live, as I have described it, 'otherwise' than modernity but not outside it."[1]

That said, the idea of consistent development and progress within Bhabha's work must be approached with caution. In many ways, he challenges the notion of dialectical* progress in intellectual activity (that is, intellectual progress achieved through argument and counterargument until a synthesis of the two is achieved); for him, the key term is not "development" but "iteration," where each "reiteration" of ideas both consolidates and changes their central meaning. This is as true for Bhabha's career as a whole as it is for the ideas presented in *The Location of Culture*. This is not to suggest

> **❝** The minoritization of a people, no less than its 'nationalization,' exceeds the language of numbers and the majoritarian claim to a 'common good.' It must be seen for what it is: the 'other side,' the alterity, the fantasy of the national 'people-as-one' that disturbs the parochial dream of ascendant authority. **❞**
>
> Homi K. Bhabha, "Unpacking My Library ... Again"

that Bhabha's "iterative" thought has no coherence between ideas or between periods in his career. Many ideas first presented in *The Location of Culture* were taken up in later writings. Similarly, the notion of hybridity,* which is discussed throughout the book, can be seen at the heart of the more recent concept of "vernacular cosmopolitanism"* (a reaction to the West-centrism at the heart of common understandings of "cosmopolitanism," detailed by Bhabha himself, according to which there are many equally valid cultural poles across the world).

In a sense, Bhabha's work has been consistently inconsistent, returning to the same concepts and questions, especially the nature of colonial identity, but from many different theoretical standpoints and sets of evidence.

Integration

The title *The Location of Culture* is a perfect introduction to Homi K. Bhabha's intellectual project. The seemingly self-confident assertion that a subject as notoriously slippery as culture can be located spatially and conceptually leads the reader to pause even before the book is opened. Should the title be taken at face value as introducing an easily read map of human culture, or have we in fact been invited to read between these (and perhaps all other) lines? Going past the title and into the text, it soon becomes apparent that it is the latter approach that Bhabha advocates. *The Location of Culture* is a complex "map" that actually leads the reader away from fixed conceptual destinations and "dislocates" the very notion of culture.

The book is important within Bhabha's body of work for three reasons. First, it demonstrates that from the mid-1980s onwards he had been pursuing certain common lines of inquiry and consistently developing and testing the various theoretical approaches that would become associated with his work (based on the interplay between poststructuralism,* literary criticism, and psychoanalysis*). Second, when his work is considered as a whole, rather than a scattering of discrete articles across journals in different disciplinary and geographical locations, it becomes much easier to appreciate "the degree to which Bhabha challenges the vision of his predecessors in the postcolonial field and those of Fanon* and Said* in particular."[2] Finally, it was the publication of *The Location of Culture* that brought Bhabha into full public view and extended the critical engagement with his work well beyond the field of postcolonialism.

Significance

It was not until *The Location of Culture* that clear lines of inquiry and the development of key theoretical terms within Bhabha's body of work became apparent to a broad readership. Bhabha established a fundamental theoretical language in which postcolonialism could express itself. This still provides the framework for contemporary studies in literature and beyond. Naturally, other theorists, such as Gayatri Spivak,* have extended and nuanced Bhabha's concepts, but they have not moved beyond them.

The publication of *The Location of Culture* also signaled the beginning of an often-vigorous critical reaction that has marked much of Bhabha's career ever since. The lasting influence and importance of Bhabha's body of work is fiercely contested, with some claiming it is "a stunning contribution to literary, historical and cultural studies"[3] and others seeing it as a damaging "substitution of poststructuralist* linguistic manipulation for historical and social explanation."[4] However, even Bhabha's most ardent critics acknowledge his effect on the development of postcolonial theory from the 1980s onwards.

Beyond this debate, the influence of Bhabha's body of work can be traced in the common currency that many of his critical terms (such as cultural hybridity,* mimicry,* the uncanny* and the Third Space*) enjoy in disciplines as distinct as literary theory and geography.

NOTES

1   Homi K. Bhabha, *The Location of Culture* (Abingdon: Routledge Classics, 2004), 18.

2   Bart Moore-Gilbert, *Postcolonial Theory: An Introduction* (London: Verso, 1994), 114.

3   Henry Louis Gates Jr, dustjacket quote for the 2004 Routledge Classics edition of *The Location of Culture*.

4   Arif Dirlik, *The Postcolonial Aura: Third World Criticism in the Age of Global Capitalism* (Oxford: Oxford University Press, 1997), 78, n. 7.

SECTION 3
IMPACT

THE FIRST RESPONSES

KEY POINTS

- Bhabha's work has been criticized for being written in inaccessible language and for placing reading and writing as forms of resistance ahead of direct action (mass protests or civil disobedience, for example).

- Bhabha argues that the "obscurity" of his work actually keeps it fresh, and helps generate new ideas by forcing readers to be more engaged in their reading.

- Bhabha's work continues to inspire academics in many fields, in many different ways.

Criticism

Several aspects of the essays in Homi K. Bhabha's *The Location of Culture* attracted initial attention. Many critics, among them the Turkish-born historian Arif Dirlik,* suggested that Bhabha's analysis often got lost among complex terminology and linguistic flourishes, and never fully addressed his object of study: "[Bhabha] has proven himself to be something of a master of political mystification and theoretical obfuscation, of a reduction of social and political problems to psychological ones, and of the substitution of poststructuralist* linguistic manipulation for historical and social explanation."[1]

For Dirlik, the complexity of Bhabha's writing is an impediment to both the comprehension of his intentions and to their successful realization. For others, Bhabha's difficult prose avoids the creation of what the British postcolonial* theorist Robert Young* calls a "meta-language" (an overarching set of structures or ideas) that would be as inflexible as the discourse* he analyzes, and that

> **❝**Bhabha's work engages with complex theoretical issues in tangential rather than systematic ways, and the essays in this collection are written in a style which is quite ostentatious in its elaborateness of theoretical reference and arcaneness of poststructuralist technique.**❞**
>
> Gillian Rose, "The Interstitial Perspective"

would conclude, paradoxically, by "repeating the same structures of power and knowledge in relation to its material as the colonial* representation itself."[2] In other words, Bhabha's work creates an open language that encourages reinterpretations and challenges, rather than an authoritative text that future thinkers must adhere to.

Others have criticized Bhabha for making reading the most potent act of social and political activism. The literary and cultural theorist Benita Parry* argued that Bhabha's overemphasis on reading and textual dissent downplays activism in the real world; for her, the political possibilities of engaging in discourse actually neutralize dissent.[3]

Responses

Although Bhabha rarely engaged directly with his critics, in a 2008 interview he explained, "As far as what others have done with my work, I'm not known to respond to critics directly in their terms. I don't engage people in great public debates; I take what I need, learn as much as I can and move on to do the next thing."[4]

Nevertheless, Bhabha has responded often, if indirectly, to criticism of his allegedly obscure writing style. In an interview soon after the publication of *The Location of Culture*, he acknowledged that any book that was so complex "that people cannot respond to it and meditate on it and use it"[5] could be classified as a failure. He went on to suggest, however, that some of the most criticized passages of the book were actually the most important because they were the most experimental, in that they extended the boundaries of his (and his readers') thought: "That moment of obscurity contains ... the limit of what I have thought, the horizon that has not as yet been reached, yet it brings with it an emergent move in the development of a concept that must be marked, even if it can't be elegantly or adequately realized."[6]

Bhabha responded directly to the suggestion that psychoanalysis* was a fundamentally Eurocentric tool by pointing out that one of the earliest university chairs in psychoanalysis was established at the University of Kolkata in India. Kolkatan psychoanalysis, Bhabha notes, is neither an Austrian import nor an Indian original, but rather a "vernacular" reading of the original that represents what he calls "a deep unpicking of ... those thoughts and those forms of textuality and then a reconstellation of them."[7] So even the theories that Bhabha uses are, in some ways, a demonstration of the hybridity* he analyzes.

Conflict and Consensus

Criticism of Bhabha's work came from such varied ideological and geographical quarters—with many of the harshest readings coming from other postcolonial thinkers—that it is difficult to talk of a "critical consensus." The suggestion in Hardt and Negri's influential *Empire* (2000), that the world was beyond the kind of colonial/postcolonial oppositions analyzed in Bhabha's text, can certainly be read as a challenge to the analytical relevance of Bhabha's work—and to postcolonialism in general.

Incidences of direct responses to critics are uncommon in Bhabha's writing. Nevertheless, when the 2001 terrorist attacks (9/11*) on the United States provoked people in the US and beyond to think in the language of "them" and "us," Bhabha suggested that

Hardt and Negri's dismissal of the binary oppositions that had preoccupied postcolonialism was "to claim too much too soon."[8]

Some of the early debate around *The Location of Culture* did inspire Bhabha to become involved in the almost constant reconsideration and reinterpretation of his own theories and ideas. In "Unpacking My Library … Again" (1996), for example, Bhabha reiterates the notion of hybridity under the new term of "vernacular cosmopolitanism."*

While no overall consensus has emerged between Bhabha and his critics, it is clear that *The Location of Culture* remains an important and influential intervention in a field still growing and developing.

NOTES

1   Arif Dirlik, *The Postcolonial Aura: Third World Criticism in the Age of Global Capitalism* (Oxford: Oxford University Press, 1997), 333.

2   Robert Young, *White Mythologies: Writing History and the West* (London: Routledge, 2004), 146.

3   Benita Parry, "Signs of Our Times: Discussion of Homi K. Bhabha's *The Location of Culture,*" *Third Text* 28/29 (1994): 15.

4   Eleanor Byrne, *Homi K. Bhabha* (Basingstoke: Palgrave Macmillan, 2009), 140.

5   W .J. T. Mitchell, "Translator Translated (Interview with Cultural Theorist Homi K. Bhabha)," *Artforum* 33, no. 7 (1995): 80.

6   Mitchell, "Translator Translated," 80.

7   Byrne, *Bhabha* 142.

8   Homi K. Bhabha, "Making Difference: Homi K. Bhabha on the Legacy of the Culture Wars," *Artforum* 46, no. 8 (2003): 237.

THE EVOLVING DEBATE

KEY POINTS

- Bhabha's work contributed to the "linguistic turn"*—
  a renewed focus in the field of philosophy on the
  relationship between language and knowledge; in cultural
  studies, it is associated with inquiry into the ways in
  which experience is represented in textual forms.

- Since its publication *The Location of Culture* has
  helped to redefine and shape the entire field of
  postcolonial* studies.

- Bhabha's work continues to generate new debates in
  postcolonial studies and beyond.

Uses and Problems

Homi K. Bhabha's innovative combination of the insights provided by the approach to cultural analysis known as poststructuralism,* the therapeutic method of psychoanalysis,* and his application of the theoretical tools derived from them to questions concerning authority and the legacies of colonialism* has had a lasting legacy of its own. This can be traced both generally and more specifically.

In general, Bhabha's work helped provoke a shift from thinking about life or actions themselves to considering the ways in which those things might be represented. *The Location of Culture* is much more interested in language than action, forming part of what has been described as "the linguistic turn in cultural studies."[1] The linguistic turn is understood as a change in emphasis from the documentation of lived experiences towards the analysis of the ways in which those experiences are represented, narrated, and discussed.

> **"**Bhabha is a member of what has come to be known as the 'Holy Trinity' of postcolonial theory, the remaining members being Edward Said and Gayatri Chakravorty Spivak. Bhabha builds on Said's work, but takes it in new directions.**"**
>
> Robert Young, *Colonial Desire: Hybridity in Theory, Culture, and Race*

A vivid example of this refocusing on writing and representation can be read early in the first chapter of *The Location of Culture*, in which Bhabha claims that "history is *happening*," not on battlefields or barricades, but "within the pages of theory, within the systems and structures we construct to figure the passage of the historical."[2] For Bhabha, history is not what happens, but how it is represented.

More specifically, many of the key terms that Bhabha developed have become common currency in other disciplines. To take just one example, his notion of hybridity* as an original mixing of influences making the idea of cultural "purity" difficult to sustain has been taken up by several scholars of globalization* (the increasing convergence of economic, political, and cultural ties and systems across continents). The global communications scholar Marwan M. Kraidy,* for example, argues that hybridity has become the central "cultural logic" of globalization because it points to common cultural blends, "thus offering foreign media and marketers transcultural wedges for forging affective links between their commodities and local communities."[3] More optimistically, the cultural studies specialist Jan Nederveen Pieterse* argues that an interpretation of globalization as hybridization shines a light on the presence of "Other"* cultures already at the core of metropolitan cultures; in this way, he challenges the idea that globalization is a one-way act of "Westernization."[4]

Schools of Thought

It is commonly accepted that Bhabha is one of the founding figures of postcolonialism. Although the genesis of this intellectual school actually predates the publication of *The Location of Culture*, beginning with the work of Edward Said,* Bhabha's theoretical conceptions and challenges played a vital part in stimulating the development of the field. However, it was only with the appearance of *The Location of Culture* that the author's many lines of inquiry (previously spread throughout a variety of specialist academic journals) came together in a coherent intellectual project with which others could engage. Bhabha offers a theoretical language and framework for postcolonial scholars, and terminology such as "hybrid" is now standard across the discipline.

His project, however, called the whole concept of distinct disciplines into question. Indeed, Bhabha suggested that schools of thought can actually become "prisons of method, whether by the misplaced dogmatism [rigidity of thought] of practitioners or in response to institutional and disciplinary hegemonies [dominance]."[5]

Nonetheless, a trend has emerged that follows Bhabha's insistence on the primacy of the text as a point of contest, challenge, or rebellion. This runs parallel to, and indeed now often blends with, "the general project of anti-colonial critique as it is taken up by poststructuralist or new historicist* thinkers."[6] "New historicism" is a type of literary criticism developed during the 1980s that argues that texts are manifestations of their political and cultural contexts. Consequently, the text must be read in context, and contexts can be rediscovered through historical texts. Along with the US literary critic Stephen Greenblatt's* *Renaissance Self-Fashioning* (1980), Bhabha's work, in particular *The Location of Culture*, is a foundational text in scholarship such as this.

In Current Scholarship

Though Bhabha's ideas have spread across disciplinary boundaries, the majority of current scholarship engaging with his ideas lies within the field of English literature. There are two main strands to this work. The first is an extension of Bhabha's own project of literary criticism, with the theoretical innovations of *The Location of Culture* being applied to new texts. These are not necessarily confined to works produced in or by colonized cultures. For example, one recent analysis of the nineteenth-century novelist Emily Brontë's* *Wuthering Heights* uses Bhabha's concepts to show that for the character Heathcliff "the mimicry becomes a tool of protest against his oppressors."[7]

The second main strand of engagement with Bhabha is in the study of minority literatures. In particular, recent work has attempted to show how cultures that we might think of as colonial do not always act as colonized. For example, there has been a recovery of the way in which native Canadian writers represent tribal culture, "a world view based in a particular Indigenous community without comparing it to the white world."[8] Here, it is Bhabha's work on marginality that is most useful. By "marginality," Bhabha and those writers following him mean the way in which some elements of a hybrid culture are given less prominence than others—in this case, indigenous literature that does not deal with colonization has been given less attention than literature that does.

Both of these strands of scholarship accept the central ideas of Bhabha's work, and develop the key concepts laid out in *The Location of Culture*. Arguably, the main engagement with Bhabha today is the work of extending his ideas to new places, literatures, and peoples.

NOTES

1   Benita Parry, "Signs of Our Times: Discussion of Homi K. Bhabha's *The Location of Culture*," *Third Text* 28/29 (1994): 5.

2   Homi K. Bhabha, *The Location of Culture* (Abingdon: Routledge Classics, 2004), 37.

3   Marwan M .Kraidy, *Hybridity, or the Cultural Logic of Globalization* (Philadelphia, PA: Temple University Press, 2005), 148.

4   Jan Nederveen Pieterse, "Globalization as Hybridization," *International Sociology* 9, no. 2 (1994).

5   Bhabha, *Location of Culture*, unnumbered first page.

6   Stephen Slemon, "Modernism's Last Post," in *A Postmodern Reader*, ed. Joseph Natoli and Linda Hutcheon (New York: SUNY Press, 1993), 427.

7   Sayantika Chakraborty, "Otherization and Ambivalence of Heathcliff in Wuthering Heights," *Asian Journal of Multidisciplinary Studies* 3, no. 8 (2015), 119–23 (121).

8   Debashee Dattaray, "Travelling Knowledges" in *Vernacular Worlds, Cosmopolitan Imagination*, ed. Stephanos Stephanides and Stavros Karayanni (Leiden: Brill, 2015), 88

MODULE 11
IMPACT AND INFLUENCE TODAY

KEY POINTS

- While *The Location of Culture* is a foundational text, many of its ideas have gone through new iterations.
- The work's central ideas challenge those who seek broad or universal narratives of global change and conflict.
- Postcolonial* critics such as Gayatri Spivak* have responded to these narratives by reasserting the importance of local applications of global ideas.

Position

When considering the current relevance of Homi K. Bhabha's *The Location of Culture* it is important to recognize that many of the ideas initially presented in the book have undergone several subsequent reiterations and subtle adaptations. It is this process of change that has kept them relevant and useful even 20 years after first publication. The concept of "hybridity,"* for example, that was so central in the 1994 publication, had been recast as the related concept of "vernacular cosmopolitanism"* in the preface to the new edition in 2004. Similarly, Bhabha's 1994 reflections on "cultural difference" have been given several practical applications in his writings on multiculturalism[1] (larger communities composed of different constituent cultures) and his contribution to the debate on human rights in an international context.[2]

The debate stimulated by the book extends well beyond any limited disciplinary borders. Some of the key concepts have been deployed in contexts as varied as the World Economic Forum* and in revisions of the national school curricula to think about the way

> **"** Harvard University's Homi K. Bhabha is one of the most influential postcolonial theoreticians of diasporic★ culture and multiculturalism, and has sought to deconstruct various narratives of nationality that serve to naturalize Third World countries as subordinate to the West. **"**
>
> Anthony Elliott and Charles Lemert, *Introduction to Contemporary Social Theory*

in which minority cultures might be represented; they have been used to challenge the perception that international politics might be interpreted according to the uncompromising binaries of "Order" and "Disorder"; and they have given insights into the ways in which contemporary cultural productions, such as the self-deprecating jokes of minority communities, are in fact forms of mimicry★ produced by their status as minorities, even if they themselves are not colonized.[3]

Interaction

Perhaps the primary theoretical debate in which the *Location of Culture* can be placed is that of universality. This comes from two directions: firstly, postcolonial scholars themselves, who have moved away from the analysis of colonialism★ as simple acts of occupation and oppression towards an understanding of colonialism by other forms, notably cultural assimilation (the process by which a dominant culture absorbs a weaker culture); and secondly, critics of postcolonialism who argue that the universality of capitalism★ makes divisions such as East and West irrelevant.

Proponents of the first position tend to focus on the role of the United States, which they see as a cultural, rather than a territorial, empire. They focus on the way in which "a ubiquitous American presence, through the dissemination of goods, commodities and the American way of life" has become "a new form of colonization."[4] Bhabha does not address this kind of colonization directly, not least because it is much more evident now than when he was writing. However, his key theoretical ideas can be applied to it—the idea of mimicry, for example, can help scholars think about the way in which global brands such as Coca-Cola are adapted by local practices, especially when this is ironic, or a call to resist consumption.

The ideas contained within (and developed from) *The Location of Culture* also represent a significant challenge to Marxist★ thought, which relies for its analysis on an assumption that capitalism is a universal driving force in global development. Bhabha's arguments about the essential instability of identity★ and belief systems extended to ideologies such as Marxism: "Denying any essentialist logic ... is a strong, principled argument against political separatism of any color, and cuts through the moralism that usually accompanies such claims."[5] Moreover, his discussion and practice of a type of argument that could be described as "non-dialectical"★ (in that it does not progress from argument and counterargument to a final synthesis of the two) represents a serious challenge to all thought systems such as Marxism, for which dialectics are central.

The Continuing Debate

The debate around *The Location of Culture* tends to return to the question of whether analyses of colonized cultures can coexist with analyses of global systems. In a recent work, the social scientist Vivek Chibber★ has offered a critique of postcolonial thought by replacing the territorial acquisition of nation-states with the global development of the economic system of capitalism. He attempted to "expose the flaws of [postcolonial theory]" and even to "displace it," by arguing that capitalism is a universal system that assimilates both Western and non-Western thought.[6] In many ways, such universalizing theories are an attack on Bhabha's careful description of the spaces in between cultures and societies. If Chibber is correct, and capitalism ultimately erases the difference between all cultures by making them consumer-driven societies, then there are no longer "in-between" spaces in which Bhabha's ideas of hybridity or mimicry might operate. In a scathing review of the work, citing Bhabha's *The Location of Culture* among other key postcolonial texts, Gayatri Spivak★ argued that Chibber is mistaken in seeing colonialism as simply the direct action of nations, and claims he has "a need to misrepresent this field in order to make his point."[7]

Bhabha remains an influential figure within postcolonial studies, and much of his work is still accepted and used as the jumping-off point for further postcolonial research, or for attacks on that field as a whole.

NOTES

1 Homi K. Bhabha, "Liberalism's Sacred Cow: A Response to Susan Okin's 'Is Multiculturalism Bad for Women?' *Boston Review,* October 1, 1997, accessed November 15, 2015, www.bostonreview.net/forum/ multiculuralism-bad-women/homi-k-bhabha-liberalisms-sacred-cow.

2 Homi K. Bhabha, "On Writing Rights," in *Globalizing Rights: The Oxford Amnesty Lectures 1999*, ed. Matthew J. Gibney (Oxford: Oxford University Press, 2003).

3 See Homi K. Bhabha, "Joking Aside: The Idea of a Self-Critical Community," in *Modernity, Culture and "the Jew,"* ed. Bryan Cheyette and Laura Marcus (Cambridge: Polity Press, 1998).

4 Vander Casaqui, "Coca-Colonization," in *The Wiley Blackwell Encyclopaedia of Consumption and Consumer Studies*, ed. Daniel Thomas Cook and J Michael Ryan (Chichester: Wiley, 2015), 89.

5 Homi K. Bhabha, *The Location of Culture* (Abingdon: Routledge Classics, 2004), 39–40.

6 Vivek Chibber, *Postcolonial Theory and the Specter of Capital* (New York: Verso, 2013), 276.

7 Gayatri Chakravorty Spivak, "*Postcolonial Theory and the Specter of Capital,*" *Cambridge Review of International Affairs* 27, no. 1 (2014): 184–98 (184).

MODULE 12
WHERE NEXT?

KEY POINTS

- Bhabha's text is a foundational work in postcolonial studies,* and still generates interest and debate today.
- The text has been adapted by thinkers in a number of fields outside of postcolonialism, such as architecture.
- The range of ideas contained in *The Location of Culture*, and the way they have generated further ideas and debates, makes the work seminal.

Potential

Homi K. Bhabha's *The Location of Culture* remains enduringly influential. In part this is because Bhabha himself remains conspicuous both within and beyond his discipline. Students coming to Bhabha's thought for the first time, as well as those more familiar with his work who wish to return to the source, will often look to *The Location of Culture*. In this sense, it is a classic work within postcolonial studies.

What is more, the fact that the ideas are presented in the book as a process of constant development has ensured their relevance has not faded. This ongoing iteration, alteration, and adaptation of ideas is precisely what Bhabha advocated and demonstrated in the original essays, within which seemingly decisive concepts soon reveal their instability (the fluidity between his notions of mimicry* and hybridity* is a noteworthy example of this). For some critics, this was evidence that Bhabha's writing lacked substance beyond its "neologisms [newly coined words] and Latinate buzzwords."[1] For others, this conceptual fluidity was evidence that Bhabha practiced

> 66 Although many of his most influential writings were originally published during the 1980s, Bhabha is very much a thinker for the twenty-first century. 99
>
> David Huddard, *Homi K. Bhabha*

what he preached, refused to let his terms "reify into static concepts" (i.e., he refused to allow his terms to take on a definite, fixed meaning, thinking that would limit their potential) and thus avoided the fatal pitfall of repeating the same structures of power and knowledge that he criticized in colonial discourse.*[2] As a consequence, *The Location of Culture* has proved remarkably fertile territory for generating new applications of critical theory, particularly in other disciplines, and it is likely this will continue.

Future Directions

Although *The Location of Culture* remains influential in current debate both within and beyond its most obvious disciplinary borders, it is not appropriate yet to talk of the text's "disciples." Bhabha did not seek to create followers of his work; rather, he intended that *The Location of Culture* would inspire its readers to adapt or play with his concepts in ways that he had not considered.

A number of intellectuals have taken Bhabha at his word and engaged critically with the ideas contained within his book, offering many avenues for future thought. Literary scholars are still exploring the full implications of Bhabha's notion of "cultural difference," and in particular how its presence in a text can reveal something of social organization. For example, in her readings of Native American fictional courtroom dramas in Canada, the theorist Maggie Ann Bowers* uses Bhabha to explain the deployment of "other"* belief systems in ways that challenge the authority of the nation's justice system.[3]

Outside of literature, the work of architects such as Felipe Hernández* demonstrates the rich potential of Bhabha's text as a part of social and urban planning. Hernández argues that Bhabha's ideas of ambivalence,* hybridity, and the Third Space* ought to be used to challenge "the [dominant] normality" of Western architectural theory and practice, which has relegated "minoritarian architectures"—the architecture of minority cultures or of "minor" building traditions—to the status of unsophisticated "others."[4] Hernández is, in effect, calling for the literary and cultural insights of *The Location of Culture* to be applied to architecture and physical spaces. Some contemporary architects have even begun to do this. The prominent Indian architect Rahul Mehrotra* has started using Bhabha's concepts of pedagogical and performative nationality to think about the way in which space in the city can be developed. It can, he argues, either be centrally planned (pedagogical) or have its use determined organically by the people living in it (performative).[5]

Summary

The Location of Culture and its author merit special critical attention for a number of reasons. First, by bringing together and building upon the work of Frantz Fanon* and Edward Said,* who are considered to have inaugurated the field of postcolonial studies, Bhabha fundamentally challenged the normality, stability, and authority of colonial interpretations and representations of colonized countries and their inhabitants. Through his amalgamation of Said and the poststructuralists'* focus on discourse, and Fanon and the psychoanalysts'* insistence on the ambivalence* of colonial understandings of identity, Bhabha constructed an innovative theoretical framework with which to challenge the overconfident self-perception and projection of colonial thinkers and writers.

The ideas put forward in *The Location of* Culture have been influential both within and beyond postcolonial thought. Bhabha's focus on discourse and his insistence on the meticulous reading and cross-reading of the textual aspects and qualities of culture, for example, was both part of and an important stimulus to the so-called "cultural turn" that took place in several academic disciplines in the 1980s and 1990s. Geographers, architects, and educators are just some of the groups who are now beginning to realize the full value of Bhabha's thought in addressing the problems and challenges in their own disciplines. The adaptability and usefulness of Bhabha's ideas beyond postcolonialism may well turn out to be *The Location of Culture*'s enduring legacy.

NOTES

1   Mark Crispin Miller, quoted in Emily Eakin, "Harvard's Prize Catch, a Delphic Postcolonialist," *New York Times*, November 17, 2001, accessed November 15, 2015, http://www.nytimes.com/2001/11/17/arts/harvard-s-prize-catch-a-delphic-postcolonialist.html?pagewanted=all.

2   Robert J. C. Young, *White Mythologies: Writing History and the West* (London: Routledge, 2004), 146.

3   Maggie Ann Bowers, "Incommensurability and Survivance: Native North American Literature and Federal Law," *Journal of Postcolonial Writing* 46, no. 5 (2010).

4   Felipe Hernández, *Bhabha for Architects* (London: Routledge, 2010), 12.

5   Rahul Mehrotra, foreword to *Rethinking the Informal City: Critical Perspectives from Latin America*, ed. Felipe Hernández, Peter Kellett, and Lea K. Allen (Oxford: Berghahn Books, 2010), xi–xiv.

GLOSSARIES

GLOSSARY OF TERMS

Agency: the capacity to act according to a decision.

Ambivalence: inconsistency, contradiction.

Canon: the cultural productions (literature, art, music, and so on) of a nation that are taken as unquestionably great, and central to that nation's tradition.

Capitalism: an economic system whereby private ownership controls a country's trade and industry, with the aim of producing a profit.

Cold War: a term used for the tension between the United States and Soviet Union, owing to their opposed economic models of communism and capitalism. It stretched roughly from the end of World War II in 1945 to the collapse of the USSR in 1991.

Colonialism: the policy of claiming and exploiting "foreign" territories—an action that brings with it cultural, political, and social consequences for the colony's original inhabitants.

Communism: a political ideology that relies on the state ownership of the means of production, the collectivization of labor, and the abolition of social class.

Dialectics: a method of argument that appeals to logic and reasoned debate in the pursuit of truth. In its classical form it is based on a dialogue between thesis and counter-thesis that often leads not to the refutation of either one, but to the amalgamation of both in a synthetic, improved, solution.

Diaspora: from the Greek for "scattering" or "dispersion," this term most commonly refers to large groups of people who are displaced from their countries or regions of origin but who retain cultural or other affiliations and some collective desire for a return.

Discourse: the framework of assumptions and language inside which something is discussed and understood.

Enlightenment: an eighteenth-century intellectual movement in Europe. It emphasized individual liberty, personal freedom, religious toleration, and the development of scientific thought.

Globalization: the increasing convergence of economic, political, and cultural ties and systems across continents

Hinduism: a polytheistic religion of the Indian subcontinent with philosophical and theological texts—the Vedas—derived from Iron Age sources. Hinduism is the largest religion in India.

Hybridity: Bhabha uses the term hybridity, or "cultural hybridity," to describe the mixed nature of supposedly "original" or "authentic" identities.

Identity: a sense of self; personhood; a self-conception or individual being related to, and partly formed by, a larger community or nation.

Indian Mutiny: a series of wide-scale military and civilian uprisings against British colonial rule in India in 1857–8, largely in the north of the country. Now often referred to as the Indian Rebellion or the First War of Independence.

Liberalism: a political and social philosophy based on individual and social freedoms such as freedom of speech, religion, and association.

Liminal: a term used to describe states of transition, transformation, or uncertainty. Bhabha uses the term extensively to describe (among other things) people and cultures who are marginalized from Western modernity but who welcome this marginality and the freedom it affords them.

Linguistic turn: a renewed focus in the field of philosophy on the relationship between language and knowledge. In cultural studies, it is associated with inquiry into the ways in which experience is represented in textual forms and a change in emphasis from the documentation of lived experiences towards the analysis of the ways in which those experiences are represented, narrated, and discussed.

Marxism: an analytical model that sees class conflict, and economic conflict more broadly, as the cause of social and cultural change.

Mimicry: a term used by Bhabha to describe the theatrical imitation of socio-cultural customs by the colonized.

New historicism: a type of literary criticism developed during the 1980s that argues that texts are manifestations of their political and cultural contexts. Consequently, the text must be read in context, and contexts can be rediscovered through historical texts.

9/11: the attacks on the World Trade Center in New York, and the Pentagon in Virginia on September 11, 2001. Planes were flown into the two towers, causing them to collapse, with significant civilian casualties. Al-Qaeda, an extremist Muslim group, took responsibility for the attack.

Ontology: the philosophical study of being, existence, and the essences of things. It deals with what beings or entities can be said to exist, how they are related to each other, and how they can be categorized according to their fundamental similarities and differences.

The "Other": that which is different from, usually opposite to, ourselves. "Other" people or things are defined by their differences, usually as a negative of the positive images associated with the "self." The concept can be seen at both an individual and national level.

Parsi: the descendants of Zoroastrians who arrived in Mumbai as exiles from Persia in the eighth century and subsequently sought to position themselves between Hindu and Muslim cultures.

Postcolonialism: an academic discipline concerned with uncovering and criticizing the cultural (and political-economic) legacies of colonial rule.

Poststructuralism: where "structuralist" theory offers an understanding of human culture as seen through the structures found in language, poststructuralist thought rejects the coherence of such structures, and instead proposes a much more "disordered" understanding of human experience.

Psychoanalysis: a therapeutic method that claims childhood experiences are critical to adult mental life, and that human behavior is inspired by irrational and unconscious motivation.

Subaltern: in postcolonial thought, the term "subaltern" refers to individuals and groups who are socially, culturally, politically, or geographically on the very perimeters of colonialism's predominant world view.

Subaltern Studies Group: a group of international scholars committed to writing the subaltern history of India; that is, a history that focuses on the masses rather than the elites.

Third Space: a term used in cultural geography (the study of the cultural impact of place), urban studies, and sociology (the study of human society) to describe a space that exists alongside the public and private spheres, demonstrating characteristics of both.

Uncanny: a term used by the pioneering psychoanalyst Sigmund Freud for a phenomenon in which something that is usually familiar is made subtly different, so that it becomes disturbing or distressing.

UNESCO (United Nations Educational Scientific and Cultural Organization): a department of the United Nations founded with the aim of promoting peace through international collaboration in spheres such as science, the preservation of heritage, culture, and education.

Vernacular cosmopolitanism: a development of the idea of hybridity by Bhabha himself. It is a reaction to the West-centrism that is at the heart of common understandings of cosmopolitanism. It holds that there are many equally valid cultural poles across the world.

World Economic Forum: a Swiss-based international institution founded to further cooperation between the state-owned and private spheres.

PEOPLE MENTIONED IN THE TEXT

Maggie Ann Bowers is a critic of Canadian and transatlantic women's writing. She has a particular interest in forms of narrative in postcolonial fiction.

Emily Brontë (1818–48) was one of four literary siblings. She is now best known for her only novel, *Wuthering Heights*, considered a classic of English literature.

Vivek Chibber (b. 1966) is a professor of sociology at New York University. He has written widely on state-building, especially in postcolonial states, as well as postcolonial theory.

Joseph Conrad (1857–1924) was a Polish British author. He is considered an important precursor of modernist literature in English, in particular for novels such as *Heart of Darkness* (1899).

Jacques Derrida (1930–2004) was a French philosopher who developed the influential mode of semiotic analysis known as "deconstruction." His most notable books are *Of Grammatology* (1976), *Speech and Phenomena* (1973), and *Writing and Difference* (1978).

Arif Dirlik (b. 1940) is a Turkish-born historian specializing in Chinese social and political history. He gained notoriety for his vitriolic attacks on the field of postcolonial studies and the works of some of its major proponents.

Terry Eagleton (b. 1943) is one of the United Kingdom's most influential literary theorists. He has published over 40 theoretical and critical texts, including *Literary Theory: an Introduction* (1983).

Frantz Fanon (1925–61) was a French Martiniquan psychiatrist, philosopher, and revolutionary whose *The Wretched of the Earth* (1961) asserts colonized people's right to use violence in the pursuit of independence.

Fernando Ortiz Fernández (1881–1969) was a Cuban anthropologist and ethnographer, interested in the origins of Cuban culture and nationality. He also helped uncover the links between Cuba and Africa.

E. M. Forster (1879–1970) was a British novelist, short-story writer, and essayist. The novel that brought him widespread public recognition, *A Passage to India* (1924), explores the prejudices and fears that fueled European colonialism in India.

Michel Foucault (1926–84) was a French philosopher and social theorist. His work challenged master narratives of society, such as the development of law and sexuality. He is known in particular for *Discipline and Punish* (1975) and *The Order of Things* (1966).

Sigmund Freud (1856–1939) was an Austrian neurologist and founder of the discipline of psychoanalysis. His major books include *The Interpretation of Dreams* (1899) and *Three Essays on the Theory of Sexuality* (1905).

Francis Fukuyama (b. 1952) is a senior fellow at Stanford University. He works on public policy and international relations, and is most famous for his book *The End of History and the Last Man* (1992), which argued that the era of conflict between ideologies was over.

Mohandas Karamchand Ghandi (1869–1948) was a leading figure in the struggle for Indian independence. He advocated nonviolent forms of protest, and is now usually known by the honorific title "Mahatma," meaning "venerable" in Sanskrit, the scriptural language of Hinduism.

Stephen Greenblatt (b. 1943) is an American literary critic and professor of the humanities at Harvard University.

Ranajit Guha (b. 1923) is a historian of South Asia, now most famous as the founder of the Subaltern Studies Group.

Kris D. Gutierrez is a professor at the Berkeley School of Education. She uses the concept of the Third Space to examine the way in which learning environments can be best designed.

Felipe Hernández (b. 1971) is an architect, and lectures in architecture at the University of Cambridge. He has particular expertise in cities in the developing world.

David Huddart is a postcolonial theorist and assistant professor of English literature at the Chinese University of Hong Kong. His major publications are *Homi K. Bhabha* (2006) and *Postcolonial Theory and Autobiography* (2008).

Marwan M. Kraidy is a US-based scholar of global communication and Arab media and politics who has written extensively on local and national strategies for confronting globalization.

Jacques Lacan (1901–81) was a French psychoanalyst and psychiatrist who made a significant contribution to poststructuralism.

Rahul Mehrotra (b. 1959) is an Indian architect, founder of RMA Architects, and a professor of urban design at Harvard University. He is especially interested in how architecture can help with conservation and urban-planning in India.

Bart Moore-Gilbert (b. 1952) is a British academic and political campaigner. Notable works by him include *Kipling and Orientalism* (1986) and *Postcolonial Life-Writing: Culture, Politics, and Self-Representation* (2009).

Benita Parry is a South African-born literary and cultural theorist who has published widely in postcolonial studies and the literatures of colonialism and imperialism.

Jan Nederveen Pieterse (b. 1946) is a US-based Dutch cultural-studies specialist who has made significant contributions to notions of globalization and cultural hybridity, notably in *Global Mélange: Globalization and Culture* (2003) and *Globalization or Empire?* (2004).

Edward Said (1935–2003) was a Palestinian American literary theorist and founding-figure of postcolonialism. He is best known for his book *Orientalism* (1978).

Edward Soja (1940–2015) was known for his work on spatial geography, and also wrote on urban planning in the developing world.

Gayatri Chakravorty Spivak (b. 1942) is an Indian literary theorist, philosopher, and foundational contributor to postcolonial thought. She is perhaps best known for her essay "Can the Subaltern Speak?" (1988).

Robert J. C. Young (b. 1950) is a British postcolonial theorist and historian. He is the author of *White Mythologies: Writing History and the West* (1990).

WORKS CITED

WORKS CITED

Afzal-Khan, Fawzia. "Surviving Theory: A Conversation with Homi K. Bhabha." In *The Pre-Occupation of Postcolonial Studies*, edited by Fawzia Afzal-Khan and Kalpana Seshadri-Crooks, 369–79. Durham, NC: Duke University Press, 2000.

Bhabha, Homi K. "Foreword: Remembering Fanon—Self, Psyche and the Colonial Condition." In Frantz Fanon, *Black Skin, White Masks*, i–xxiv. London: Pluto Press, 1986.

— — —. "Unpacking My Library ... Again." In *The Postcolonial Question*, edited by Iain Chambers and Lidia Curti, 199–211. London: Routledge, 1996.

— — —. "Liberalism's Sacred Cow: A Response to Susan Okin's 'Is Multiculturalism Bad for Women?'" *Boston Review,* October 1, 1997. Accessed November 15, 2015, www.bostonreview.net/forum/multiculuralism-bad-women/homi-k-bhabha-liberalisms-sacred-cow.

— — —. "Joking Aside: The Idea of a Self-Critical Community." In *Modernity, Culture and "the Jew,"* edited by Bryan Cheyette and Laura Marcus, xv–xx. Cambridge: Polity Press, 1998.

— — —. "Making Difference: Homi K. Bhabha on the Legacy of the Culture Wars." *Artforum* 46, no. 8 (2003): 73–5, 234–7.

— — —. "On Writing Rights." In *Globalizing Rights: The Oxford Amnesty Lectures 1999*, edited by Matthew J. Gibney, 162–83. Oxford: Oxford University Press, 2003.

— — —. *The Location of Culture*. Abingdon: Routledge Classics, 2004.

Bowers, Maggie Ann. "Incommensurability and Survivance: Native North American Literature and Federal Law." *Journal of Postcolonial Writing* 46, no. 5 (2010): 457–67.

Byrne, Eleanor. *Homi K. Bhabha*. Basingstoke: Palgrave Macmillan, 2009.

Casaqui, Vander. "Coca-Colonization." In *The Wiley Blackwell Encyclopaedia of Consumption and Consumer Studies,* edited by Daniel Thomas Cook and J. Michael Ryan, 89–90. Chichester: Wiley, 2015.

Chakraborty, Sayantika. "Otherization and Ambivalence of Heathcliff in Wuthering Heights." *Asian Journal of Multidisciplinary Studies* 3, no. 8 (2015): 119–23.

Chibber, Vivek. *Postcolonial Theory and the Specter of Capital*. New York: Verso, 2013

Dattaray, Debashee. "Travelling Knowledges." In *Vernacular Worlds, Cosmopolitan Imagination*, edited by Stephanos Stephanides and Stavros Karayanni, 87–101. Leiden: Brill, 2015.

Dirlik, Arif. *The Postcolonial Aura: Third World Criticism in the Age of Global Capitalism*. Oxford: Oxford University Press, 1997.

Eakin, Emily. "Harvard's Prize Catch, a Delphic Postcolonialist." *New York Times*, November 17, 2001. Accessed November 15, 2015. http://www.nytimes.com/2001/11/17/arts/harvard-s-prize-catch-a-delphic-postcolonialist.html?pagewanted=all.

Fanon, Frantz. *The Wretched of the Earth*. New York: Grove Press, 1961.

Fukuyama, Francis. "The End of History." *The National Interest* (1989), 3–18.

Gutiérrez, K. D. "Developing a Sociocritical Literacy in the Third Space." *Reading Research Quarterly* 43, no. 2 (2008): 148–64.

Hardt, Michael, and Antonio Negri. *Empire*. Cambridge, MA: Harvard University Press, 2000.

Hernández, Felipe. *Bhabha for Architects*. London: Routledge, 2010.

Huddart, David. *Homi K. Bhabha*. London: Routledge, 2006.

Hunter, James Davison. *Culture Wars: The Struggle to Define America*. New York: Basic Books, 1991.

Kraidy, Marwan M. *Hybridity, or the Cultural Logic of Globalization*. Philadelphia, PA: Temple University Press, 2005.

Maitland, Sarah. "'In-Between' a Rock and a 'Third Space'? On the Trouble with Ambivalent Metaphors of Translation." *Translation Studies,* 2015, 1–9. Accessed November 15, 2015. doi: 10.1080/14781700.2015.1085432.

Mehrotra, Rahul. Foreword to *Rethinking the Informal City: Critical Perspectives from Latin America*, edited by Felipe Hernandez, Peter Kellett, and Lea K. Allen. Oxford: Berghahn Books, 2010.

Mitchell, W. J. T. "Translator Translated (Interview with Cultural Theorist Homi Bhabha)." *Artforum* 33, no. 7 (1995): 80–4.

Moore-Gilbert, Bart. *Postcolonial Theory: An Introduction*. London and New York: Verso, 1994.

Parry, Benita. "Signs of Our Times: Discussion of Homi K. Bhabha's *The Location of Culture.*" *Third Text* 28/29 (1994): 5–24.

Pieterse, Jan Nederveen. "Globalization as Hybridization." *International Sociology* 9, no. 2 (1994): 161–84.

Slemon, Stephen. "Modernism's Last Post." In *A Postmodern Reader*, edited by Joseph Natoli and Linda Hutcheon. New York: SUNY Press, 1993.

Soja, Edward W. *Thirdspace: Journeys to Los Angeles and Other Real-and-Imagined Places.* Oxford: Blackwell, 1996.

Spivak, Gayatri Chakravorty. "Can the Subaltern Speak?" In *Marxism and the Interpretation of Culture,* edited by Cary Nelson and Lawrence Grossberg, 271–313. Urbana: University of Illinois Press, 1988.

———. "Postcolonial Theory and the Specter of Capital." *Cambridge Review of International Affairs* 27, no. 1 (2014): 184–98

Young, Robert J. C. *Colonial Desire: Hybridity in Theory, Culture, and Race.* London: Routledge, 1995.

———. *White Mythologies: Writing History and the West.* London: Routledge, 2004.

THE MACAT LIBRARY
BY DISCIPLINE

AFRICANA STUDIES

Chinua Achebe's *An Image of Africa: Racism in Conrad's Heart of Darkness*
W. E. B. Du Bois's *The Souls of Black Folk*
Zora Neale Huston's *Characteristics of Negro Expression*
Martin Luther King Jr's *Why We Can't Wait*
Toni Morrison's *Playing in the Dark: Whiteness in the American Literary Imagination*

ANTHROPOLOGY

Arjun Appadurai's *Modernity at Large: Cultural Dimensions of Globalisation*
Philippe Ariès's *Centuries of Childhood*
Franz Boas's *Race, Language and Culture*
Kim Chan & Renée Mauborgne's *Blue Ocean Strategy*
Jared Diamond's *Guns, Germs & Steel: the Fate of Human Societies*
Jared Diamond's *Collapse: How Societies Choose to Fail or Survive*
E. E. Evans-Pritchard's *Witchcraft, Oracles and Magic Among the Azande*
James Ferguson's *The Anti-Politics Machine*
Clifford Geertz's *The Interpretation of Cultures*
David Graeber's *Debt: the First 5000 Years*
Karen Ho's *Liquidated: An Ethnography of Wall Street*
Geert Hofstede's *Culture's Consequences: Comparing Values, Behaviors, Institutes and Organizations across Nations*
Claude Lévi-Strauss's *Structural Anthropology*
Jay Macleod's *Ain't No Makin' It: Aspirations and Attainment in a Low-Income Neighborhood*
Saba Mahmood's *The Politics of Piety: The Islamic Revival and the Feminist Subjec*t
Marcel Mauss's *The Gift*

BUSINESS

Jean Lave & Etienne Wenger's *Situated Learning*
Theodore Levitt's *Marketing Myopia*
Burton G. Malkiel's *A Random Walk Down Wall Street*
Douglas McGregor's *The Human Side of Enterprise*
Michael Porter's *Competitive Strategy: Creating and Sustaining Superior Performance*
John Kotter's *Leading Change*
C. K. Prahalad & Gary Hamel's *The Core Competence of the Corporation*

CRIMINOLOGY

Michelle Alexander's *The New Jim Crow: Mass Incarceration in the Age of Colorblindness*
Michael R. Gottfredson & Travis Hirschi's *A General Theory of Crime*
Richard Herrnstein & Charles A. Murray's *The Bell Curve: Intelligence and Class Structure in American Life*
Elizabeth Loftus's *Eyewitness Testimony*
Jay Macleod's *Ain't No Makin' It: Aspirations and Attainment in a Low-Income Neighborhood*
Philip Zimbardo's *The Lucifer Effect*

ECONOMICS

Janet Abu-Lughod's *Before European Hegemony*
Ha-Joon Chang's *Kicking Away the Ladder*
David Brion Davis's *The Problem of Slavery in the Age of Revolution*
Milton Friedman's *The Role of Monetary Policy*
Milton Friedman's *Capitalism and Freedom*
David Graeber's *Debt: the First 5000 Years*
Friedrich Hayek's *The Road to Serfdom*
Karen Ho's *Liquidated: An Ethnography of Wall Street*

John Maynard Keynes's *The General Theory of Employment, Interest and Money*
Charles P. Kindleberger's *Manias, Panics and Crashes*
Robert Lucas's *Why Doesn't Capital Flow from Rich to Poor Countries?*
Burton G. Malkiel's *A Random Walk Down Wall Street*
Thomas Robert Malthus's *An Essay on the Principle of Population*
Karl Marx's *Capital*
Thomas Piketty's *Capital in the Twenty-First Century*
Amartya Sen's *Development as Freedom*
Adam Smith's *The Wealth of Nations*
Nassim Nicholas Taleb's *The Black Swan: The Impact of the Highly Improbable*
Amos Tversky's & Daniel Kahneman's *Judgment under Uncertainty: Heuristics and Biases*
Mahbub Ul Haq's *Reflections on Human Development*
Max Weber's *The Protestant Ethic and the Spirit of Capitalism*

FEMINISM AND GENDER STUDIES

Judith Butler's *Gender Trouble*
Simone De Beauvoir's *The Second Sex*
Michel Foucault's *History of Sexuality*
Betty Friedan's *The Feminine Mystique*
Saba Mahmood's *The Politics of Piety: The Islamic Revival and the Feminist Subjec*t
Joan Wallach Scott's *Gender and the Politics of History*
Mary Wollstonecraft's *A Vindication of the Rights of Woman*
Virginia Woolf's *A Room of One's Own*

GEOGRAPHY

The Brundtland Report's *Our Common Future*
Rachel Carson's *Silent Spring*
Charles Darwin's *On the Origin of Species*
James Ferguson's *The Anti-Politics Machine*
Jane Jacobs's *The Death and Life of Great American Cities*
James Lovelock's *Gaia: A New Look at Life on Earth*
Amartya Sen's *Development as Freedom*
Mathis Wackernagel & William Rees's *Our Ecological Footprint*

HISTORY

Janet Abu-Lughod's *Before European Hegemony*
Benedict Anderson's *Imagined Communities*
Bernard Bailyn's *The Ideological Origins of the American Revolution*
Hanna Batatu's *The Old Social Classes And The Revolutionary Movements Of Iraq*
Christopher Browning's *Ordinary Men: Reserve Police Batallion 101 and the Final Solution in Poland*
Edmund Burke's *Reflections on the Revolution in France*
William Cronon's *Nature's Metropolis: Chicago And The Great West*
Alfred W. Crosby's *The Columbian Exchange*
Hamid Dabashi's *Iran: A People Interrupted*
David Brion Davis's *The Problem of Slavery in the Age of Revolution*
Nathalie Zemon Davis's *The Return of Martin Guerre*
Jared Diamond's *Guns, Germs & Steel: the Fate of Human Societies*
Frank Dikotter's *Mao's Great Famine*
John W Dower's *War Without Mercy: Race And Power In The Pacific War*
W. E. B. Du Bois's *The Souls of Black Folk*
Richard J. Evans's *In Defence of History*
Lucien Febvre's *The Problem of Unbelief in the 16th Century*
Sheila Fitzpatrick's *Everyday Stalinism*

The Macat Library By Discipline

Eric Foner's *Reconstruction: America's Unfinished Revolution, 1863-1877*
Michel Foucault's *Discipline and Punish*
Michel Foucault's *History of Sexuality*
Francis Fukuyama's *The End of History and the Last Man*
John Lewis Gaddis's *We Now Know: Rethinking Cold War History*
Ernest Gellner's *Nations and Nationalism*
Eugene Genovese's *Roll, Jordan, Roll: The World the Slaves Made*
Carlo Ginzburg's *The Night Battles*
Daniel Goldhagen's *Hitler's Willing Executioners*
Jack Goldstone's *Revolution and Rebellion in the Early Modern World*
Antonio Gramsci's *The Prison Notebooks*
Alexander Hamilton, John Jay & James Madison's *The Federalist Papers*
Christopher Hill's *The World Turned Upside Down*
Carole Hillenbrand's *The Crusades: Islamic Perspectives*
Thomas Hobbes's *Leviathan*
Eric Hobsbawm's *The Age Of Revolution*
John A. Hobson's *Imperialism: A Study*
Albert Hourani's *History of the Arab Peoples*
Samuel P. Huntington's *The Clash of Civilizations and the Remaking of World Order*
C. L. R. James's *The Black Jacobins*
Tony Judt's *Postwar: A History of Europe Since 1945*
Ernst Kantorowicz's *The King's Two Bodies: A Study in Medieval Political Theology*
Paul Kennedy's *The Rise and Fall of the Great Powers*
Ian Kershaw's *The "Hitler Myth": Image and Reality in the Third Reich*
John Maynard Keynes's *The General Theory of Employment, Interest and Money*
Charles P. Kindleberger's *Manias, Panics and Crashes*
Martin Luther King Jr's *Why We Can't Wait*
Henry Kissinger's *World Order: Reflections on the Character of Nations and the Course of History*
Thomas Kuhn's *The Structure of Scientific Revolutions*
Georges Lefebvre's *The Coming of the French Revolution*
John Locke's *Two Treatises of Government*
Niccolò Machiavelli's *The Prince*
Thomas Robert Malthus's *An Essay on the Principle of Population*
Mahmood Mamdani's *Citizen and Subject: Contemporary Africa And The Legacy Of Late Colonialism*
Karl Marx's *Capital*
Stanley Milgram's *Obedience to Authority*
John Stuart Mill's *On Liberty*
Thomas Paine's *Common Sense*
Thomas Paine's *Rights of Man*
Geoffrey Parker's *Global Crisis: War, Climate Change and Catastrophe in the Seventeenth Century*
Jonathan Riley-Smith's *The First Crusade and the Idea of Crusading*
Jean-Jacques Rousseau's *The Social Contract*
Joan Wallach Scott's *Gender and the Politics of History*
Theda Skocpol's *States and Social Revolutions*
Adam Smith's *The Wealth of Nations*
Timothy Snyder's *Bloodlands: Europe Between Hitler and Stalin*
Sun Tzu's *The Art of War*
Keith Thomas's *Religion and the Decline of Magic*
Thucydides's *The History of the Peloponnesian War*
Frederick Jackson Turner's *The Significance of the Frontier in American History*
Odd Arne Westad's *The Global Cold War: Third World Interventions And The Making Of Our Times*

LITERATURE

Chinua Achebe's *An Image of Africa: Racism in Conrad's Heart of Darkness*
Roland Barthes's *Mythologies*
Homi K. Bhabha's *The Location of Culture*
Judith Butler's *Gender Trouble*
Simone De Beauvoir's *The Second Sex*
Ferdinand De Saussure's *Course in General Linguistics*
T. S. Eliot's *The Sacred Wood: Essays on Poetry and Criticism*
Zora Neale Huston's *Characteristics of Negro Expression*
Toni Morrison's *Playing in the Dark: Whiteness in the American Literary Imagination*
Edward Said's *Orientalism*
Gayatri Chakravorty Spivak's *Can the Subaltern Speak?*
Mary Wollstonecraft's *A Vindication of the Rights of Women*
Virginia Woolf's *A Room of One's Own*

PHILOSOPHY

Elizabeth Anscombe's *Modern Moral Philosophy*
Hannah Arendt's *The Human Condition*
Aristotle's *Metaphysics*
Aristotle's *Nicomachean Ethics*
Edmund Gettier's *Is Justified True Belief Knowledge?*
Georg Wilhelm Friedrich Hegel's *Phenomenology of Spirit*
David Hume's *Dialogues Concerning Natural Religion*
David Hume's *The Enquiry for Human Understanding*
Immanuel Kant's *Religion within the Boundaries of Mere Reason*
Immanuel Kant's *Critique of Pure Reason*
Søren Kierkegaard's *The Sickness Unto Death*
Søren Kierkegaard's *Fear and Trembling*
C. S. Lewis's *The Abolition of Man*
Alasdair MacIntyre's *After Virtue*
Marcus Aurelius's *Meditations*
Friedrich Nietzsche's *On the Genealogy of Morality*
Friedrich Nietzsche's *Beyond Good and Evil*
Plato's *Republic*
Plato's *Symposium*
Jean-Jacques Rousseau's *The Social Contract*
Gilbert Ryle's *The Concept of Mind*
Baruch Spinoza's *Ethics*
Sun Tzu's *The Art of War*
Ludwig Wittgenstein's *Philosophical Investigations*

POLITICS

Benedict Anderson's *Imagined Communities*
Aristotle's *Politics*
Bernard Bailyn's *The Ideological Origins of the American Revolution*
Edmund Burke's *Reflections on the Revolution in France*
John C. Calhoun's *A Disquisition on Government*
Ha-Joon Chang's *Kicking Away the Ladder*
Hamid Dabashi's *Iran: A People Interrupted*
Hamid Dabashi's *Theology of Discontent: The Ideological Foundation of the Islamic Revolution in Iran*
Robert Dahl's *Democracy and its Critics*
Robert Dahl's *Who Governs?*
David Brion Davis's *The Problem of Slavery in the Age of Revolution*

The Macat Library By Discipline

Alexis De Tocqueville's *Democracy in America*
James Ferguson's *The Anti-Politics Machine*
Frank Dikotter's *Mao's Great Famine*
Sheila Fitzpatrick's *Everyday Stalinism*
Eric Foner's *Reconstruction: America's Unfinished Revolution, 1863-1877*
Milton Friedman's *Capitalism and Freedom*
Francis Fukuyama's *The End of History and the Last Man*
John Lewis Gaddis's *We Now Know: Rethinking Cold War History*
Ernest Gellner's *Nations and Nationalism*
David Graeber's *Debt: the First 5000 Years*
Antonio Gramsci's *The Prison Notebooks*
Alexander Hamilton, John Jay & James Madison's *The Federalist Papers*
Friedrich Hayek's *The Road to Serfdom*
Christopher Hill's *The World Turned Upside Down*
Thomas Hobbes's *Leviathan*
John A. Hobson's *Imperialism: A Study*
Samuel P. Huntington's *The Clash of Civilizations and the Remaking of World Order*
Tony Judt's *Postwar: A History of Europe Since 1945*
David C. Kang's *China Rising: Peace, Power and Order in East Asia*
Paul Kennedy's *The Rise and Fall of Great Powers*
Robert Keohane's *After Hegemony*
Martin Luther King Jr.'s *Why We Can't Wait*
Henry Kissinger's *World Order: Reflections on the Character of Nations and the Course of History*
John Locke's *Two Treatises of Government*
Niccolò Machiavelli's *The Prince*
Thomas Robert Malthus's *An Essay on the Principle of Population*
Mahmood Mamdani's *Citizen and Subject: Contemporary Africa And The Legacy Of Late Colonialism*
Karl Marx's *Capital*
John Stuart Mill's *On Liberty*
John Stuart Mill's *Utilitarianism*
Hans Morgenthau's *Politics Among Nations*
Thomas Paine's *Common Sense*
Thomas Paine's *Rights of Man*
Thomas Piketty's *Capital in the Twenty-First Century*
Robert D. Putman's *Bowling Alone*
John Rawls's *Theory of Justice*
Jean-Jacques Rousseau's *The Social Contract*
Theda Skocpol's *States and Social Revolutions*
Adam Smith's *The Wealth of Nations*
Sun Tzu's *The Art of War*
Henry David Thoreau's *Civil Disobedience*
Thucydides's *The History of the Peloponnesian War*
Kenneth Waltz's *Theory of International Politics*
Max Weber's *Politics as a Vocation*
Odd Arne Westad's *The Global Cold War: Third World Interventions And The Making Of Our Times*

POSTCOLONIAL STUDIES

Roland Barthes's *Mythologies*
Frantz Fanon's *Black Skin, White Masks*
Homi K. Bhabha's *The Location of Culture*
Gustavo Gutiérrez's *A Theology of Liberation*
Edward Said's *Orientalism*
Gayatri Chakravorty Spivak's *Can the Subaltern Speak?*

PSYCHOLOGY

Gordon Allport's *The Nature of Prejudice*
Alan Baddeley & Graham Hitch's *Aggression: A Social Learning Analysis*
Albert Bandura's *Aggression: A Social Learning Analysis*
Leon Festinger's *A Theory of Cognitive Dissonance*
Sigmund Freud's *The Interpretation of Dreams*
Betty Friedan's *The Feminine Mystique*
Michael R. Gottfredson & Travis Hirschi's *A General Theory of Crime*
Eric Hoffer's *The True Believer: Thoughts on the Nature of Mass Movements*
William James's *Principles of Psychology*
Elizabeth Loftus's *Eyewitness Testimony*
A. H. Maslow's *A Theory of Human Motivation*
Stanley Milgram's *Obedience to Authority*
Steven Pinker's *The Better Angels of Our Nature*
Oliver Sacks's *The Man Who Mistook His Wife For a Hat*
Richard Thaler & Cass Sunstein's *Nudge: Improving Decisions About Health, Wealth and Happiness*
Amos Tversky's *Judgment under Uncertainty: Heuristics and Biases*
Philip Zimbardo's *The Lucifer Effect*

SCIENCE

Rachel Carson's *Silent Spring*
William Cronon's *Nature's Metropolis: Chicago And The Great West*
Alfred W. Crosby's *The Columbian Exchange*
Charles Darwin's *On the Origin of Species*
Richard Dawkin's *The Selfish Gene*
Thomas Kuhn's *The Structure of Scientific Revolutions*
Geoffrey Parker's *Global Crisis: War, Climate Change and Catastrophe in the Seventeenth Century*
Mathis Wackernagel & William Rees's *Our Ecological Footprint*

SOCIOLOGY

Michelle Alexander's *The New Jim Crow: Mass Incarceration in the Age of Colorblindness*
Gordon Allport's *The Nature of Prejudice*
Albert Bandura's *Aggression: A Social Learning Analysis*
Hanna Batatu's *The Old Social Classes And The Revolutionary Movements Of Iraq*
Ha-Joon Chang's *Kicking Away the Ladder*
W. E. B. Du Bois's *The Souls of Black Folk*
Émile Durkheim's *On Suicide*
Frantz Fanon's *Black Skin, White Masks*
Frantz Fanon's *The Wretched of the Earth*
Eric Foner's *Reconstruction: America's Unfinished Revolution, 1863-1877*
Eugene Genovese's *Roll, Jordan, Roll: The World the Slaves Made*
Jack Goldstone's *Revolution and Rebellion in the Early Modern World*
Antonio Gramsci's *The Prison Notebooks*
Richard Herrnstein & Charles A Murray's *The Bell Curve: Intelligence and Class Structure in American Life*
Eric Hoffer's *The True Believer: Thoughts on the Nature of Mass Movements*
Jane Jacobs's *The Death and Life of Great American Cities*
Robert Lucas's *Why Doesn't Capital Flow from Rich to Poor Countries?*
Jay Macleod's *Ain't No Makin' It: Aspirations and Attainment in a Low Income Neighborhood*
Elaine May's *Homeward Bound: American Families in the Cold War Era*
Douglas McGregor's *The Human Side of Enterprise*
C. Wright Mills's *The Sociological Imagination*

The Macat Library By Discipline

Thomas Piketty's *Capital in the Twenty-First Century*
Robert D. Putman's *Bowling Alone*
David Riesman's *The Lonely Crowd: A Study of the Changing American Character*
Edward Said's *Orientalism*
Joan Wallach Scott's *Gender and the Politics of History*
Theda Skocpol's *States and Social Revolutions*
Max Weber's *The Protestant Ethic and the Spirit of Capitalism*

THEOLOGY

Augustine's *Confessions*
Benedict's *Rule of St Benedict*
Gustavo Gutiérrez's *A Theology of Liberation*
Carole Hillenbrand's *The Crusades: Islamic Perspectives*
David Hume's *Dialogues Concerning Natural Religion*
Immanuel Kant's *Religion within the Boundaries of Mere Reason*
Ernst Kantorowicz's *The King's Two Bodies: A Study in Medieval Political Theology*
Søren Kierkegaard's *The Sickness Unto Death*
C. S. Lewis's *The Abolition of Man*
Saba Mahmood's *The Politics of Piety: The Islamic Revival and the Feminist Subject*
Baruch Spinoza's *Ethics*
Keith Thomas's *Religion and the Decline of Magic*

COMING SOON

Chris Argyris's *The Individual and the Organisation*
Seyla Benhabib's *The Rights of Others*
Walter Benjamin's *The Work Of Art in the Age of Mechanical Reproduction*
John Berger's *Ways of Seeing*
Pierre Bourdieu's *Outline of a Theory of Practice*
Mary Douglas's *Purity and Danger*
Roland Dworkin's *Taking Rights Seriously*
James G. March's *Exploration and Exploitation in Organisational Learning*
Ikujiro Nonaka's *A Dynamic Theory of Organizational Knowledge Creation*
Griselda Pollock's *Vision and Difference*
Amartya Sen's *Inequality Re-Examined*
Susan Sontag's *On Photography*
Yasser Tabbaa's *The Transformation of Islamic Art*
Ludwig von Mises's *Theory of Money and Credit*

Printed in the United States
by Baker & Taylor Publisher Services